W9-CKL-997

THE *WEHRMACHT* AND GERMAN REARMAMENT

THE *WEHRMACHT* AND GERMAN REARMAMENT

by
Wilhelm Deist

Foreword by
A. J. Nicholls

University of Toronto Press
Toronto and Buffalo

Published in the United Kingdom 1981 by
The Macmillan Press Ltd

First published in Canada
and the United States of America 1981 by
University of Toronto Press
Toronto and Buffalo

ISBN 0 8020 2423 8

Printed in Hong Kong

Contents

Foreword

For some years scholars in Germany have been conducting intensive research into their own military history between the two World Wars. It is important that the fruits of their research should be made available to English readers. Dr Deist is uniquely qualified to fulfil this task. As a distinguished member of the Institute for Military Historical Research at Freiburg-im-Breisgau he has immersed himself in the voluminous documentation available on this subject, and has made substantial contributions to German historical literature in the field. In 1978 he was a Visiting Leverhulme Fellow at St Antony's College, Oxford, where he delivered a most original and stimulating series of lectures. The present volume is based on those lectures, though it has been revised and expanded.

In discussions about the origins of the Second World War reference is always made to the level of rearmament achieved by the Germans between 1933 and 1939. The victories of the Nazi Armies in the first two years of the War would have been inconceivable without a very remarkable growth in Germany's military strength since the era of the Weimar Republic, when she had been so weak that even defensive operations against Poland could not be regarded with any sort of optimism. In 1919 the Germans had had to accept the humiliating restrictions of the Versailles Treaty, which held their army to a level of 100,000 men on long-term enlistment; abolished their military air force and placed such restrictions on their navy as to render it incapable of all but the most elementary defensive tasks. Despite some erosions of the Treaty during the 1920s, Germany was still a very weak military nation when Hitler took office in January 1933. Only six years were needed to transform her into a power capable of defeating France and Poland, chase the British army out of the European continent and inflict grievous losses on the Soviet Union.

Yet the Nazi rearmament programme still remains a matter of controversy. Historians have been divided over its extent and the purpose behind it. Figures are sometimes produced which seem to

show that in 1939 the Germans were not well equipped by
comparison with their adversaries. Some historians have claimed
that the German economy was not particularly orientated towards
war and that investment was mainly for peaceful purposes.[1] Others
stress the overriding priority given to armaments by Hitler and the
economic distortions which arose from it.[2]

The first merit of Dr Deist's admirable book is that it finally
disposes of any doubts about the massive extent of Nazi Germany's
rearmament in the first six years of the Third Reich. Here we find
set out the enormously rapid – not to say hectic – expansion of all
three armed services between 1933 and 1939. As with many other
aspects of Nazi economic and social policy, the ground had been
prepared by the governments of Brüning, von Papen and von
Schleicher in the depression period, but Hitler's appearance as
Chancellor altered the tempo and the scope of their policies. More
and more ambitious objectives were set for the Army. At the same
time the new German *Luftwaffe* was being created and the Navy was
preparing itself to attain parity with France before going on to a
programme which would enable it to threaten British naval
superiority.[3] In the autumn of 1939 Germany mobilised an army of
two and three quarter million men in 103 divisions. This included
six armoured divisions and four motorised infantry divisions. The
Air Force had over 4000 front line aircraft of modern design with
302 operational squadrons trained and ready for combat.[4] The
Navy was, of course, less advanced, and in no condition to wage war
against Britain, but it had increased its personnel strength five-fold
since 1933 and was equipped almost exclusively with modern
warships. The naval budget of 1939 was twelve times that of 1932
and expenditure had risen steadily to this peak from 1933.[5] Clearly
a tremendous amount of investment and labour had been necessary
to produce this result.

There were, however, aspects of the German rearmament
programme which have still led historians to doubt its purpose, even
if they accept the monumental nature of the achievement itself.
Rearmament appeared to be in 'breadth' rather than 'depth' and
the armed forces were certainly not prepared for a long war which
would require major stockpiles of military materials. Since Hitler
himself is known to have been opposed to a cautious, long-term
approach to the problem of rearmament,[6] it seemed plausible that
the Nazis deliberately opted for a strategy of short, sharp conflicts –
so-called '*Blitzkrieg*' operations – rather than a long war of attrition.

Here again, Hitler's originality and the crucial influences of his own personality were seen to be demonstrated. Yet here again the issue is complicated by conflicting evidence. Hitler never really spelled out his '*Blitzkrieg*' strategy, and the timing of his expansionist policy was clearly affected by pressures of an economic and administrative kind over which the Führer himself had no overriding control. As a result, a rather unreal conflict has arisen between those who see the warlike policies of the Third Reich as largely the outcome of Hitler's personal influence and those who prefer a more mechanistic explanation based on pressures arising from inconsistent economic policies and the rivalry of competing bureaucratic Empires.[7]

Dr Deist's account in this book makes us realise that there is really no need to adopt exclusive positions on this issue. The fact is that Hitler's persistent impatience for military strength, and his desire to use it to expand Germany's territory, was one factor in a dynamic process; inter-service rivalry and the ambitious plans of the military were others. At different times one or the other might be of greater significance, but taken together they added up to an explosive mixture which made Nazi aggression inevitable.

The German Army had, of course, never been willing to accept the Versailles Treaty, and it shared this view with most German political leaders in the Weimar Republic. Even in 1928 – a year of apparent peace and stability for Germany's new democracy – the Defence Ministry obtained cabinet approval of plans for a mobilisable army 16 divisions strong, as well as some stockpiling of war materials. This plan was so successful that in 1932 a second programme was adopted which envisaged creating an army of major proportions by 1938. The army's leaders were determined not to be restrained by any international agreement on disarmament. Initially, Defence Minister Blomberg and Foreign Minister Neurath were, if anything, more determined in their refusal to compromise with the Western Powers over disarmament than was Hitler, who was prepared to be flexible, if only for tactical purposes.[8] However, right from the beginning of his period in office Hitler encouraged the Army to go ahead with plans for expansion, and this was very important in unleashing the pent-up energies of the military leaders. They fully shared the enthusiasm of their new political masters for the restoration of Germany's position as a great power. By December 1933 they were producing plans for a peacetime army of 300,000 with a mobilised strength of 63 divisions.

It is important to note that this particularly ambitious scheme was produced partly in response to a perceived threat from a potential rival to the Army in the shape of Röhm's brown-shirted para-military formation, the SA. The Army leaders wished to demonstrate their own zeal and give themselves more authority with which to repel Röhm, who seemed intent on extending his power into the military sphere. The Generals were only too willing to help Hitler destroy Röhm, and became his accomplice in the notorious blood purge of 30 June 1934, carried out by Himmler's SS with logistical support from the Army. Almost immediately afterwards – on Hindenburg's death – German soldiers took a personal oath of loyalty to Hitler.

The ambitious expansion programme upon which the Army had embarked would be impossible without flagrant breaches of the Versailles Treaty. Here we see in operation a dynamic process which gathered its own momentum as it went along. The Army leaders wanted to be able to free themselves from the restraints of Versailles to enable them to face hostile neighbours in the field of battle. But to gain this strength they had to take risks which raised the likelihood of war. Hence from December 1933 it was obvious that conscription would be necessary – a breach of the Treaty which could not be covered up. The month of March 1935 saw Hitler announce the creation of a military air force and the introduction of conscription. These were measures presaged by the rearmament programme already decided upon by the relevant authorities. In this respect Hitler's actions were the logical outcome of military policies. Similarly, the decision to remilitarise the Rhineland in March 1936 was entirely consistent with Army planning, even if the actual *coup* itself was the work of Hitler and created nervousness in the High Command. It had become clear that in the event of war the French could not be held back in the Rhineland long enough to enable the Army to secure the Rhine, and that would leave the Ruhr – the hub of the German armaments industry – vulnerable to attack. The remilitarisation of the Rhineland was, therefore, indispensable if the Generals' plans for a mobilised army of 63 divisions were to be implemented.[9]

Once into the Rhineland, however, new opportunities were opened up for even more grandiose military expansion. Schemes were now put in train for a mobilised army of over $3\frac{1}{2}$ million men by 1940 – a far larger force than Germany put into the field in 1914.

The cost of maintaining up-to-date equipment for such an army would be enormous,[10] and raised the obvious likelihood that it would have to be used in combat soon after it had been brought up to the levels envisaged in the plan. However important Hitler's prompting was in accelerating the armaments programme, therefore, it is clear that the programme itself helped create a situation in which war was made probable, and the optimum date for that war would be the turn of the year 1939/40.[11]

This also fitted in with Hitler's requirements for the German economy as set out in the Nazi Four Year Plan.[12] Where historians have sometimes been misled is in the assumption that an armaments programme and an economic policy which gave overriding priority to rearmament, was necessarily a co-ordinated, rationally organised economic system. This was very far from being the case. As Dr Deist points out, the military armaments programmes were uncoordinated so far as the three armed services were concerned and quite unrelated to any realistic assessment of what burdens the German economy could sustain over an extended period. This itself was a major factor in producing – willy nilly – the so-called '*Blitzkrieg*' strategy. Armament in depth could not be achieved without long-term planning, effective economic co-ordination and clearly defined military priorities. Political expediency and departmental selfishness precluded such an ideal arrangement. Each service pressed ahead to create the largest possible front-line force in the shortest possible time. The Army and the Air Force attained this objective by September 1939. Even then, they were only able to do so as the result of Hitler's bloodless conquests in Austria and Czechoslovakia. Dr Deist's account illustrates once again the crucial importance of the Munich settlement for Hitler's success in the early years of the war; just as Munich transformed Germany's diplomatic position and quelled nascent resistance at home, so in the armaments field it gave the Reich vital foreign exchange credits and industrial capacity, without which the *Wehrmacht* could not have been effectively equipped a year later.

Much as Dr Deist's book helps us to understand the mechanics of the Nazi war machine, it has a wider significance. Historians are realising now that national boundaries are inadequate as a framework for the understanding of modern industrial society. The role of military requirements in shaping economic policies created problems throughout the industrially developed world. They were especially acute in the 1930s and 1940s. Military and social historians in many countries are now beginning to tackle these questions and Dr Deist's book is a most valuable contribution to a discussion, the relevance of which transcends the frontiers of German – or even European – contemporary history.

A. J. Nicholls
St Antony's College

Acknowledgements

During Trinity Term 1978, as Visiting Leverhulme Fellow at St Antony's College, Oxford, I had the opportunity of delivering a series of papers on several of the themes discussed in this volume in seminars which took place at the College's West European Studies Centre. I should like to thank the College and its members for the hospitality shown to me, and in particular the Warden, Professor R. Carr and Mr A. J. Nicholls, both of whom first suggested publishing the seminar papers and who encouraged the undertaking at every stage. I am also grateful to those who participated in the seminars, especially Michael Howard of All Souls', Timothy W. Mason of St Peter's College, R. A. C. Parker of Queen's College and Michael Geyer of Ann Arbor. I trust I have been able to take due account of their suggestions and constructive criticism in the writing of this work.

The Wehrmacht *and German Rearmament* is based on research into the history of the Second World War from a German perspective, which was taken up some years ago by the Militärgeschichtliches Forschungsamt in Freiburg. The first volume to result from this research is concerned with the causes and preconditions of German war policy and was written by my colleagues Manfred Messerschmidt, Hans-Erich Volkmann, Wolfram Wette and myself. The present volume owes a great deal to the intensive discussions we conducted on the historical problems of the period leading up to the Second World War. But for the assistance of my colleagues I could not have made this contribution to the study of German rearmament. My thanks are also due to the Bundesarchiv-Militärarchiv and the Institut für Zeitgeschichte for placing the relevant documents at my disposal.

The language barrier always hinders the presentation and publicising of the results of research. I am, therefore, especially indebted to Dr Johanna Geyer-Kordesch of St Antony's College, who, alongside her own time-consuming studies, was able to give me considerable help with the linguistic presentation of the seminar papers. The text of *The* Wehrmacht *and German Rearmament* has been translated by Eveline Traynor. I have followed with admiration her untiring efforts to be faithful to the content and sense of the original. To her I owe my sincere thanks.

Finally, I am grateful to the Leverhulme Foundation, not only for making my stay in Oxford possible, but also for their willing financial support of this volume's translation.

Introduction

In his article published in 1962, the year of the Cuban Crisis, Hans Herzfeld called for more attention to be paid to the 'fundamental and total breakdown of the relationship between armaments and politics', which became evident from the beginning of the twentieth century onwards and which 'was not confined to one nation alone'.[1] As an example of the wide-ranging effects of this 'breakdown' he discussed international developments between 1919 and 1939 together with the widely varying reactions of individual nations and political systems to the catastrophe of the First World War. In Herzfeld's view, this breakdown also requires to be taken into account in any examination of the relationship between 'Politics, Army and Armament', in the history of Germany during the inter-war period. Although Herzfeld did not define the nature of this 'breakdown' in any detail, it is fairly clear that it derived, on the one hand, from a public unease which had been growing since the First World War, and which questioned the legitimacy of war as an instrument of politics; and, on the other, from the growing destructive capacity of the industrial products of an increasingly refined armaments technology together with the military possibilities this opened up.

German military historiography, which in view of the powerful tradition of official histories produced by the General Staff was only able to establish itself as an historical discipline in its own right after the Second World War,[2] has hardly touched upon the subject. Generally speaking, it seems that research into the history of the German nation state from 1870 to 1945 attributes only secondary importance to military–historical aspects. This is all the more astonishing since there is no doubt that the creation of the German Reich, its two attempts to establish hegemony in Europe and, above all, its dominant concepts of social and political order can only be explained with reference to the influence of the armed forces on the structure of the state. Of the three phases in the historical development of the German nation state, the Kaiserreich is the one which has been most often and most rewardingly studied and researched from the point of view of military history.[3] This has meant that studies on the question of militarism and the problems of continuity and contrast in German history have led to more precise although, at the same time, diverse conclusions.[4]

A great number of military historical studies also exists on the second phase of development, the Weimar period. It is a feature of the wide range of literature on the *Reichswehr*[5] during the Republic that it approaches the subject directly from contemporary controversies on the political role of the military. It is the relationship of the *Reichswehr* and its leaders to the Republic, its institutions, and cabinet and party politics which has up to now formed the focus of interest. The main concern of historians has been to determine what factors led to the failure of the first German republic. The works of Francis L. Carsten[6] and Rainer Wohlfeil[7] in the late 1960s brought this line of research to a temporary conclusion. Recent studies have tended more often to concentrate on structural questions concerning the place of the armed forces in an industrialised and technologically oriented mass society. The fundamental change in political *and* military conditions under which, following the First World War, the traditional tasks of the armed forces had to be carried out, has until now only been touched upon, although the importance of the question has of course been recognised.[8] Further research in this field will permit a more detailed study, using the *Reichswehr* as an example, of the 'breakdown', postulated by Hans Herzfeld of the relationship between politics and armaments, the causes of the breakdown, and the effects of it.

It is no surprise that the bulk of publications dealing with the history of the military in the Third Reich which appeared during the first two decades following the end of the Second World War should have been primarily concerned with the subject of 'Schuld und Verhängnis',[9] and with the extent of the *Wehrmacht*'s responsibility for the war policy and crimes of the National Socialist régime. This is not only true of the numerous memoirs which exist, but also of the countless studies on the military resistance. The extensive discussions on the peacetime years of the Third Reich were brought to a close for the time being at the end of the 1960s with the definitive work of Klaus-Jürgen Müller.[10] In contrast, however, German military–historical discussion and research into the political, military, economic and social implications of the build-up of the *Wehrmacht* up to the outbreak of war in 1939 is as yet in its infancy. Although it is true that important contributions on isolated aspects exist, notably on the ideological assimilation (*Gleichschaltung*) of the *Wehrmacht* or on the development of operational and armament planning within the *Luftwaffe* and Navy,[11] there remain some obvious gaps. To name just one example, there has been as yet virtually no detailed investigation of the development of the officer corps. The following chapters on German rearmament may, therefore, be regarded as a further contribution to a military history of the Third Reich. When set alongside the extraordinarily wide scope and importance of existing research into British armaments policy in the inter-war period, these chapters may also serve to stimulate comparative studies which might demonstrate the wider dimensions of the 'total breakdown' while at the same time illustrating the singularity of the German development.

1 Reich Defence Minister Groener and the Problem of National Defence

Until now, interest in the brief history of the *Reichswehr*, on the part of historians as well as laymen, has concentrated mainly on the transitional periods from the Kaiserreich to the Weimar Republic and from the Republic to the Third Reich. The main subject of discussion has been the political power and real political influence exercised by the Army and Navy. The conclusions drawn in the many incisive analyses which approach the subject from a political angle, have defined and still define where the armed forces fit into the overall picture of the period. There can be no doubt that the politically motivated actions of the *Reichswehr* leadership were of decisive, if not essential, importance for the first German republic. Nevertheless, concentration on research into and explanation of these aspects of the *Reichswehr*'s history has led to neglect of military developments within the armed forces and the failure to recognise their political consequences.

According to Article 160 of the Treaty of Versailles, the *Reichswehr* was to be used exclusively for the 'maintenance of order within the German territories, and as a border police'. This definition of its function, which lent the Reich's Army more the character of a police force, was never accepted in Germany, however. On the contrary, the *Reichswehr* knew that its claim to be the traditional instrument for preserving the sovereignty and authority of the State was in complete accord with the will of a large majority of the nation and its political representatives.[1]

Yet could the *Reichswehr*, under the conditions laid down by the Treaty of Versailles, do justice to this self-appointed claim? The military terms of the treaty[2] regulated the size and structure of the *Reichswehr* right down to details of equipping and arming units; and the Allies kept a close control over their observance.[3] The second

4

head of the Army Command, General von Seeckt, the dominant figure in the early history of the *Reichswehr*, saw an answer to this problem in regarding the *Reichswehr* from the outset as merely a temporary solution. As early as January 1921 he let it be understood that he regarded it as his duty to form the *Reichswehr* into the nucleus of a future, larger *Wehrmacht* which would no longer be subject to the restrictions of Versailles.[4] During the Republic's years of stability which began after the major domestic crisis of 1923, however, it soon became apparent that a revision of the military provisions of the Treaty of Versailles could not be expected within the foreseeable future. Von Seeckt's long-term plans for the distant future were no longer regarded as satisfactory by some officers in view of the pressing nature of existing circumstances.

In February 1924, Lieutenant-Colonel Joachim von Stülpnagel, Head of the Army Department at the *Truppenamt* which was in charge of affairs previously the responsibility of the proscribed General Staff, had delivered a paper to the officers at the Reich Defence Ministry entitled, 'Thoughts on the War of the Future',[5] His considerations were based on the conviction that the Reich's continued existence and development could only be secured for the long-term by renewed conflict with France. The only question was whether, and when, the *Reichswehr* would be capable of undertaking this task. In this respect, Stülpnagel was extremely realistic: 'Today, and for the foreseeable future, to start a war would be a mere heroic gesture.' He dramatically demonstrated to the officers their own impotence by pointing out that the seven existing divisions had just enough ammunition for a conflict of approximately one hour's duration. This was the beginning of the so-called 'Fronde' within the Reich Defence Ministry. The group of officers around Joachim von Stülpnagel, which included Bussche, Blomberg and Haase, no longer found Seeckt's vision of things to come realistic, given their own present lack of power. They therefore set about coming to terms with the concrete realities of the military situation, developing accordingly a concept of national defence corresponding to actual conditions. This circle was not held together by a single political conviction or strategy but by the common goal of maintaining and increasing the military efficiency of the *Reichswehr*.[6] Furthermore, there was general agreement that the *Reichswehr*, in view of increasing political stability at home, could only achieve this aim by co-operating closely with all departments of the State executive. Besides, the economic problems of rearma-

ment and the more general organisational problems of national
defence could only be solved with the aid of the civil administration.
If progress was to be achieved in these areas, there was little point in
making wide-ranging demands on matters of principle, especially
during a phase of relative political stability. Instead, it was
necessary to traverse the stony ground of statistical investigations,
interminable discussions, accepting even the smallest advantage.
This was not Seeckt's way. Thus his dismissal at the beginning of
October 1926 and the appointment of Lieutenant-General Heye as
his successor marked a decisive turning-point in the history of the
Reichswehr.[7]

The resignation of Geßler, the Reich Defence Minister of long
standing, one and a half years later was less spectacular.[8] He had
loyally served the *Reichswehr* rather than led it. In dismissing Seeckt,
Geßler had cleared the way for a new concept of national defence
which implied stronger co-operation between the *Reichswehr* and the
State executive and had taken the first hesitating steps along this
road. The cause of his own resignation was in turn a legacy of the
Seeckt era: naval Captain Lohmann's shady financial dealings on
behalf of armament measures taken in secret, illegally, and without
the government's permission. This particular form of clandestine
rearmament had proved completely inefficient. The staff changes in
the positions of Reich Defence Minister and Head of the Army
Command signalled the beginnings of an attempt to form the
Republic's military policy along new lines and on a new basis.

Geßler's successor in the office of Reich Defence Minister,
Wilhelm Groener,[9] is usually mentioned in literature on the
Reichswehr solely in his role as the initiator of the Ebert–Groener
Pact of November 1918, or in connection with the problems which
arose from the SA ban of 1932. Because of this, the outlines of his
policy during his four most decisive years of office, from January
1928 to April 1932, remain obscure. The fact is deliberately
overlooked that, with Groener, there had been appointed to the top
position in the Ministry a soldier who, more than anyone else, had
been confronted during and after the First World War with the
political, economic, technical, and military problems involved in
conducting a war.

As the son of a paymaster in a Württemberg regiment, Groener
had risen to a position in the General Staff. He was promoted from
lieutenant-colonel to Head of the Railway Section in 1912. As head
of this section he had distinguished himself. The mobilisation of

August 1914 had run smoothly under his direction, and he was regarded as a trusted advisor to both Moltke and Falkenhayn. In May 1916 he was appointed a member of the executive of the wartime Food Control Office and in autumn of the same year he took over the War Office. Under the Army High Command led by Hindenburg and Ludendorff, he was entrusted with organising and mobilising the Reich's available personnel and material resources for the war effort. In this position he had acquired an intimate knowledge of the political, moral, and above all, economic conditions necessary for conducting a war and had also established contacts, based on trust, with leaders of the Social Democratic Party which were remarkable for their time. As Ludendorff's successor in the office of First Quartermaster General, he had been given the task of winding up the lost war, which would have proceeded along different lines but for his experience. Groener's position on the Treaty of Versailles, his support for Seeckt and the General Staff officer corps at the time of the formation of the new *Reichswehr*, were and are still the subject of controversy.[10] Groener was certainly no democrat, as many of his contemporaries took him to be. He was a republican by reason rather than conviction (*Vernunftrepublikaner*), but there were few enough even of these in the higher officer corps, and in fact he served the Republic well as Minister for Railway Reconstruction between 1920 and 1923.

Despite the reputation that clung to him following the events of November 1918, his great military expertise and familiarity with the military establishment earned the new Defence Minister more respect from within and outside the *Reichswehr* than Geßler had ever enjoyed.

Groener had also participated in the extensive debate,[11] carried out in military periodicals, that centred on the question of which military lessons were to be learned from the First World War. While mass armies had created considerable problems for military leaders in the operational and tactical sphere, the advent and influence of technology had had an even greater impact on waging war. In discussing the war's history, therefore, the Schlieffen Plan and the phenomenon of the war of attrition were thoroughly dealt with.[12] Behind this, however, lay concealed a crisis of the military craft in its political and social aspects, the existence of which was scarcely articulated. In countless, detailed studies on the course taken by the Battle of the Marne in 1914[13] the main question was, what military decisions had been responsible for the failure of the Schlieffen Plan.

Intensive study of Schlieffen's thought was intended to establish whether an operational war aimed at rapid results was still conceivable and feasible in an age of mass armies. It was necessary to establish this, since the experience of the Great War with its fixed positions and the human hell caused by the static war of attrition had raised serious doubts about the military's claim to leadership. It was not the once highly esteemed qualities of leadership and the skills of the war lord and his aides that had decided the outcome of the war but the size of material and personnel resources. How vexatious the problem was felt to be, can be seen from views expressed by Groener, himself one of the strongest advocates of Schlieffen's theories. He ended his conclusions in 'The Significance of the Modern Economy for Strategy' with the question whether, 'the modern economy and its problems' might not in fact 'lead inexorably to a situation where peace would prevail'.[14]

In military and historical writings such thoughts remained peripheral. Opinion was unanimous that the economic and propaganda wars which had become adjuncts of war in the traditional sense, had been decisive for the outcome of the war. In general, however, the search for new strategies adapted to new conditions characterised by mass armies and the mass-production of war materials remained the dominant preoccupation. It is important to note, however, that the question of the relationship of means to ends was no longer raised. Yet Clausewitz had considered it of prime importance in determining the nature of any conflict, with the result that war became an instrument of politics.[15] As a rule, the war of the future was defined strictly in terms of the general means to be employed. Even when objectives were defined, the emphasis was placed, first and foremost, on proving how and by what means they could be attained militarily. Considerations of the relationship between the social and economic costs of military engagements, involving as they always did incalculable risks to the desired objective and its benefits for the country and the nation, were completely ignored. In Germany, much more than in the Anglo-Saxon countries for example, the scope of the discussion was reduced to a consideration of the problems of operational warfare. This discussion revealed that the phenomenon of war between industrialised countries had become so complex and the preconditions and effects of such a war so difficult to estimate, that intellectual appraisal was limited to isolated aspects only. In the memorandum 'The Significance of the Modern Economy for

Strategy' mentioned above, Groener, by the express acknowledgement of pacifist currents in society and reference to the pacificatory effects of modern world trade, had at least brought out the basic problem of the relationship of means to ends.

As Reich Defence Minister, Groener actively continued the new policy towards the executive of the Republic which Geßler, Heye (Head of the Army Command) and Blomberg (Head of the *Truppenamt*) had introduced. In a period of relative normalcy and stability it was the aim of this policy to maintain and improve the *Reichswehr*'s military efficiency. This was only possible if Seeckt's policy of keeping the Army at a distance from the Republican system was at least partially given up. Reich Defence Minister Geßler's exposition to the cabinet[16] of 29 November 1926 is an indication of the change of climate which accompanied this. In the presence of the Heads of the Army and Naval Command, and against a background of vehement criticism from the Social Democrats, he announced a comprehensive cabinet briefing on secret rearmament by the Head of the Army Command. The cabinet had then to decide which measures could be justified, following which the *Reichswehr* would abide by this decision. In other words, with regard to national defence, the main sphere of activity of the armed forces, the primacy of political decisions and controls was recognised. Evidence given by leading officers in the Defence Ministry in winter 1926/7 reveals[17] that it was a matter of conviction born of military necessity to abandon the distance previously shown towards the Republic and its institutions. The aim of the co-operation with the civil administration, which Geßler and Heye had instituted, was to secure politically the implementation of armaments measures for personnel and equipment. In February 1927 the Head of the Army Command reported to the cabinet under Reich Chancellor Marx on the existing secret stock of arms as well as on the present state of the border and national defence forces and of further planning regarding them.[18] The Reich Chancellor and cabinet gave him to understand that they were not at all averse to incorporating the costs of the illegal armaments measures – i.e. measures which contravened the Treaty of Versailles – in the national budget. This could only happen, however, if the section of the budget allotted for the purpose did not require the normal examination and ratification by the *Reichstag*. The solution was found in a committee consisting of one representative each from the audit office, the *Reichswehr*, and the Reich Ministry of Finance, which commenced its duties with the internal decision on the 1928 budget.[19] The cabinet of the Grand Coalition under the leadership of the Social Democrat, Müller, which took office in June 1928, also accepted the decision made the previous year to relieve the *Reichswehr* of responsibility for clandestine rearmament. On Groener's initiative in October 1928, the cabinet approved suggestions by the Committee and emphatically[20] agreed to the *Reichswehr*'s plans for armament. The factor of greatest significance here is not so much the amount of funds which were now made available for secret rearmament from the budgets of the Reich Defence Ministry and later also from those of other ministries, but rather the erosion of the parliamentary system by means of decrees. In this manner, highly explosive in its implications for both foreign and domestic politics, the *Reichstag*'s rights and capacity for controlling affairs were invalidated by the co-operation which existed between the military and the civil executive.

Taking their lead from Groener, the *Reichswehr* leadership had managed to break out of its political isolation, so that the responsibility for national defence could be transferred to the Reich's political leadership, as was appropriate, with the result that by incorporating the cost of armament into the budget, the financial preconditions were created for a slow but steady improvement in the unpromising armaments situation.

The full dimensions of the success achieved by the *Reichswehr* leadership in winning the cabinet's approval of the budget becomes apparent if one considers internal *Reichswehr* planning. With Blomberg's take-over in early January 1927, the *Truppenamt* had ambitiously set itself the task of integrating all armaments planning covering material resources into an overall programme intended to fix priorities for a period of several years. After a preparation period of almost two years the programme was approved by the Head of the Army Command on 29 September 1928. The military aim was to secure the initial provision of equipment and ammunition for a 16-division army (the so-called 'A-Army') , in addition to a limited stockpiling, and measures to improve industrial production capacity for the event of mobilisation. This aim was to be achieved by the years 1928/9 and 1932 and approximately 350 million Reichsmarks were to be spent.[21] Compared with a total *Reichswehr* budget in 1928 of 726·5 million Reichsmarks (8·6 per cent of the national budget) the 70 million Reichsmarks made available annually for armaments purposes seems relatively insignificant.[22]

But a radically new element is to be noted in the methods employed by the Army Command and *Truppenamt*. Even though naval armament and the so-called 'Air Force Armament Phase of 1927–31' were not incorporated in the armaments programme,[23] the systematic attempt to integrate the number of infinitely complex and mutually interdependent factors, involved in armament based on modern industrial production methods, into a goal-oriented programme represented a new element in the history of the German Army,[24] which can only be compared with the building of the German fleet under Tirpitz. In 1932 the more comprehensive and more efficiently co-ordinated Second Army Armaments Programme was passed to cover a period from 1933 to 1938, a fact which reveals that the process had found approval within the *Reichswehr* leadership.[25]

Groener's political importance as Reich Defence Minister can be judged not only from the success of this financially modest yet modern armaments programme but also from the fact that he made a practical effort, during the *Reichswehr*'s rearmament phase, to make it an integrated military instrument in support of revisionist policies, as Stresemann had intended.

The memorandum 'Das Panzerschiff' (pocket battleship) of November 1928, which appeared in connection with Groener's representation of the Navy's interests in the cabinet and the *Reichstag*, can be seen as a first step in this direction.[26] At the outset Groener asked what tasks the *Reichswehr* could be expected to accomplish given the existing situation. Only after a well-substantiated answer were given to this question could the function of the Navy for national defence be adequately ascertained and the question examined, whether the pocket battleship then under debate constituted a necessary and worthwhile increase in the Reich's military power. The reality of military planning, however, was only a poor reflection of these clearly defined purposes to which the individual elements of national defence were to be put.[27] The Army and Navy armaments programmes which Groener placed before the cabinet in 1928 were poorly co-ordinated and not based on any unified concept,[28] although to judge from Groener's comments in the memorandum, along with other testimony, such unity of concept was precisely what he was aiming at. He could not ignore the fact that the Navy claimed 30 per cent of the *Reichswehr* budget and that its decision in favour of pocket battleships required the expenditure of considerable sums for years to come.

If Groener desired thus to influence the military decisions of the Army and Navy leadership, this would only have been possible with the help of a military staff which could promote the interests of the overall *Wehrmacht* leadership over the particular interests of Army and Navy. In early March 1929, a new ministerial department with broad responsibility under Major-General Kurt von Schleicher was set up, against the will of the Head of the Army Command. Besides meeting the wishes of the *Reichstag*, this department had to attempt the introduction of the urgently required co-ordination of armaments.[29] It has been pointed out that the complicated planning procedures, seen especially in the Second Army Armaments Programme, greatly restricted the Head of the Army Command and the Reich Defence Minister himself in exercising a decisive influence.[30] In view of this, Groener, who had had many similar experiences when Head of the War Office during the First World War, had to endeavour to make full use of the remaining opportunities for influencing affairs, aided by the new ministerial department. Both Schleicher's ambition and the necessity of increasing ministerial influence for political and military reasons contributed to the new department's growth in power.

Another area of interest demonstrates even more clearly that Groener as Reich Defence Minister was determined to assert both his political *and* military leadership over the separate branches of the armed forces. In mid-April 1930, he signed the directive, 'The Tasks of the *Wehrmacht*', and sent it to the Heads of the Army and Naval Commands.[31] The directive had been drawn up by the Ministry's *Wehrmacht* Department. In it Groener laid down a strict framework within which the deployment of the *Reichswehr* in the near future was considered possible, and stipulated in detail the means at its disposal. Right at the outset, Groener established the paramount importance of political viewpoints in defining the tasks the armed forces were to be set and stated that their actual employment must depend on '*definite* chances of success'. From this premise he concluded that 'a responsible government might if necessary' decide '*against* military resistance', and preparatory plans e.g. for evacuation and demolition, were to be made accordingly.

The prospect of the *Reichswehr* engaging in combat was reserved for the event of domestic unrest (the 'Pieck Case' as it was coded) for clearly defined situations of self-defence and for the event of a particularly favourable international situation.

According to the directive, a situation of self-defence was one where infringement by another country's irregular forces (coded 'Korfanty') or regular units (coded 'Pilsudski') threatened a military fait accompli. The deployment of the *Reichswehr* to combat regular units was only to occur if the aggressor were 'also heavily militarily engaged elsewhere' or if resistance would 'cause the intervention of other powers and international authorities'.

A favourable political situation was only to be exploited either if pressure from a particular power constellation were to offer Germany the chance of improving her political and military situation or if such pressure gave the Reich the possibility of successfully defending its own neutrality. Finally, the employment of the *Reichswehr* could 'result from a free decision of its own, if a favourable international situation permits us to take the risk inherent in such a decision'.

Groener, however, did not only confine himself to setting down political preconditions for employing the *Reichswehr*. He also set out the shape military action should take under each of the conditions mentioned above. Here he distinguished between three modes of deployment of military power: that of the Reich's standing Army; that of the reinforced Reich Army; and that of the field army comprising the Reich Army increased three times to 21 divisions plus the border defence forces. The employment of the field army was only to be envisaged for the 'Pilsudski' case and on condition that a favourable political situation were to exist.

In an appendix to the paper, Groener formulated very broad directives for improving the *Reichswehr*'s operational capacity. He emphasised the necessity of improving the operational readiness of the Army, since it constituted the only means of power '*immediately* available to the government'. He demanded that the schedule for the mobilisation be cut, that the Army be equipped with heavy artillery and other modern weapons and that training in general be improved. As far as the field army was concerned, 'plans for its creation' were to be confined to 'what was possible in terms of available equipment and other supplies'. This was a clear statement that this area required long-term plans. The Second Armaments Programme passed in 1932 was accordingly aimed at achieving the basic equipping and further provision of six weeks' supplies for the 21-division field army by spring 1938.[32]

The substance of this document has been quoted at length because it serves as a good example of how Groener attributed to armed power the clear function of an instrument of political leadership, which has only seldom been the case in German military history in the nineteenth and twentieth centuries. The directive also marks the culmination of a development which began in the mid-1920s, in which the *Reichswehr* leadership saw itself as having to draw closer to the executive institutions of the Republic for mainly military reasons and, in return for financial and political assurance on illegal military measures, having to accept political control by the executive. As Reich Defence Minister, Groener endeavoured to extend this sphere of control by formulating clear military objectives and, by defining the possible applications of armed power, he penetrated to the heart of military leadership and control. Moreover, his appendix made it clear that priorities should be worked out for the deployment of the *Reichswehr* for the specific cases mentioned. Groener and Schleicher's department had in fact acted in accordance with the first sentence of the directive: 'The tasks set for the armed forces by the responsible political authority are to be the basis for their build-up and employment'.

Any interpretation of the directive must lead to the conclusion that it was in complete accord with the revisionist policy pursued by successive cabinets of the Republic. The security of the Reich's eastern borders, which were viewed as under threat, was to the fore in the *Reichswehr*'s operational planning. Here, too, and especially for the 'Pilsudski' case, security was regarded as dependent on the functioning of the League of Nations and admission of the latter's significance for German security policies. Nor were revisionist goals left out of the directive. An unprovoked *Reichswehr* offensive was not discounted should the risk prove a calculable one.

To evaluate properly the significance of Groener's directive within the *Reichswehr*, it is necessary to examine the ideas of the military leadership which were expressed in staff studies. Of particular importance is the series of studies in the winters of 1927/8 and 1928/9 under the direction of Blomberg.[33] In these, the *Truppenamt* and Army leaders occupied themselves primarily with the possible form and course of a war against Poland. The military outcome suggested catastrophe. In the *Truppenamt*'s winter 1927/8 studies, a four-month period of tension culminated in open conflict, which the *Reichswehr* had to engage in 'under virtually hopeless conditions'. The *Truppenamt* study tour in 1928 did nothing to change this picture. The Foreign Office representative commented, in short, that a war against Poland could be waged 'for a short time only and with further German territorial losses'. Blomberg, however, would not accept this.[34] Shortly before the conflict was about to be wound up on the German side because of a lack of ammunition, he had the League of Nations intervene and force an armistice on the Poles! Thereupon the Soviet Union attacked Poland and offered to form an alliance with Germany, which gratefully accepted; now the *Reichswehr* was in a position to terminate the conflict with attacks on a grand scale! Such wishful thinking on the part of the Military scarcely contributed to a realistic assessment of Germany's political position. On the other hand it must be recognised that as far as the assessment of military possibilities and the balance of power were concerned, the *Truppenamt* had been realistic.

Nevertheless, thanks to their taking account of all armaments measures and concrete, longer-term planning to come, it had been possible to base the studies on more or less reliable data. Thus the *Truppenamt's* assessment, that at the level of armament as at 1 April 1933 – i.e. after the completion of the first armament programme – the chances of a successful defence against a Polish attack would have considerably improved, was not without foundation.

In mid-1928 the Navy had no comparable armaments programme.[35] In contrast to the Army, the Navy had gone ahead with preparatory work for a replacement shipbuilding plan somewhat later. The decision in favour of the pocket battleship never quite lost the character of a temporary solution. The struggle for pocket battleship 'A', which was to be followed by another three, marked the beginning of a tug-of-war within and outside the executive lasting years over this, the most important object of naval rearmament.[36] Yet the operations envisaged by the naval leadership developed almost independently of the availability of ships. By the time of the autumn manoeuvres of 1926, the phase when coastal defence had been the exclusive goal had been left far behind. It was also no longer purely a case of protecting Germany's maritime supply routes. In the manoeuvres the Navy took the offensive, attacking the enemy's supply routes. This was based on the assumption that 'the sea link of an enemy in the west to one in the east' had become 'a major decisive factor for the outcome of the war'.[37] According to the manoeuvres, Germany was fighting both Poland and France. A year later the Navy had already committed two pocket battleships, which were still on the drawing board, to gaining control of the Baltic in the face of combined Polish and French naval forces.

The realistic tenor of Groener's directive of 16 April 1930 stands out in marked contrast to the background of these thoughts on military planning: the gap between his aims and those of the Army and Navy leadership seemed unbridgeable. As early as in his '*Panzerschiff*' memorandum[38] Groener had unmistakably declared: 'The thought of a major war is out of the question', and thus had indirectly characterised the Navy leadership's political conclusions and military assumptions as illusory. Both the political and military premises of the Navy's manoeuvres indicate clearly that there had been no co-ordination with the Army and that the services were obviously proceeding from the assumption that each would be able to conduct its own separate war. Groener, in contrast, had endeavoured to put an end to this obsession with his unified directive to the Army and Navy. In his memorandum he had pointed out that even the role of the pocket battleship should be derived from the detailed function specified for the Reich Navy in national defence. With the 1930 directive he had indicated how the Navy's operational intentions could be brought back into line with political and military realities.[39]

In the series of studies of 1927/8, both the Army leadership and the *Truppenamt* had endeavoured to take much greater account of the realities of the military balance of power. Yet even here the tendency to ignore the sad reality and return to a traditional, extensive operational type of warfare was unmistakable. In the winter studies of 1928/9, Blomberg as Head of the *Truppenamt* tested the chances of a war on two fronts against France and Poland whose forces were also engaged against the Soviet Union.[40] The result was no surprise. Even taking the level of armament as at 1 April 1933 as a basis, the *Reichswehr* had no more than the possibility of fighting delaying actions and, eventually, a losing battle. Yet in his memorandum of 26 March 1929, Blomberg judged the situation 'not quite as hopeless as might at first appear'. He was guided in his optimism by the conviction that 'great States have never yet tolerated military violation without offering military resistance'.[41]

In this opinion the Head of the *Truppenamt* was clearly contradicting the very basis of the military policies of the Reich Defence Minister and his department. Schleicher as head of the department had a low opinion of such prestigious military thinking which was based on self-deception and ultimately doomed to end in national catastrophe. He challenged Blomberg indirectly to 'be courageous enough . . . to admit that' there could be 'military–political complications which would render a conflict hopeless from the outset'. Blomberg could not rise to the challenge and came off the worse in this argument. He was replaced as Head of the *Truppenamt* by Hammerstein-Equord at the end of September 1929.[42]

Due to force of circumstance, Groener, who all his life considered himself a disciple of Schlieffen, had developed an extraordinarily flexible military policy which no longer bore much relation to the military and strategical maxims of the Prussian Head of the General Staff. The break with traditional ideas and convictions is most evident in his definition of the role to be played by the armed forces. This break not only resulted from the restrictions of the Treaty of Versailles but also from the extension of the concept of national defence following the experiences of the First World War. Groener spoke emphatically in favour of the involvement of other sections of the State executive in national defence,[43] but, in addition to this vast enlargement of the sphere of military influence, he still emphasised that the aims set for the military should be motivated by political considerations. The directive of April 1930 represents an attempt early on in the rearmament phase to place the relationship between political policy-making and military means as described by Clausewitz at the foundation of the *Wehrmacht*. This did not mean that Groener thought armed power ought never to be anything more than an instrument of a defensive security policy. It was his opinion, however, as far as having a military basis for an expansive foreign policy was concerned that '*definite* chances of success [were the] prerequisite' for initiating any military conflict.

At the end of Groener's period of office early in 1932, the *Reichswehr* could no longer be compared with Seeckt's *Reichswehr* as it existed at the beginning of the Republic's years of stability. Under Groener's influential direction the functional capacity of the military in terms of national defence had been decidedly improved. The *Reichswehr*'s political influence was evidenced by the fact that in October 1931 Groener, already Reich Defence Minister, took on the additional office of Reich Minister of the Interior.[44] On the basis of a modern, comprehensive concept of national defence, the armed forces now possessed a realistic theory for action as well as a medium-term armaments programme and were now able to begin to free themselves from the constraints of the Treaty of Versailles.

In contrast to Geßler, Groener took full advantage of his position of political and military control and leadership, attempting to force his will on the Army and Navy leadership. His influence depended on the continuance of the existing political stability. This precondition was however removed, at the latest, by the spectacular success of the National Socialists in the *Reichstag* elections of September 1930. At the beginning of October 1930, Groener, in an instruction to his commanders, was able to assert proudly that the *Reichswehr* leadership had been successful in 'making the *Reichswehr* the strongest element in the State', which no one could afford to 'ignore when making political decisions'.[45] Groener regarded this as a consequence of the policy pursued since 1926/7. It is revealing, however, that the Reich Defence Minister felt obliged by the Ulm *Reichswehr* trial, and in defence of this very policy, to resort to this sort of statement. Within the *Reichswehr* itself, criticism of the policy of co-operation had been directed against its first premise, the necessity of recognising the Republic, its institutions and parties as political realities.

The trial of the Ulm *Reichswehr* officers heard in the supreme court in Leipzig and the reaction to it within the *Reichswehr* revealed dangerous disagreement between the *Reichswehr* leaders and the majority of its officers.[46] Groener was compelled to defend himself in several statements against the accusation that the *Reichswehr* leaders were following a 'leftist' course and neglecting national defence. An analysis of views prevalent in the officer corps shows that the widespread criticism that existed was not necessarily based on a rejection on principle of the constitution and the republican system.[47] More important to the officer than the constitution was the reality of the State: in his view the State ought to be 'strong' and hierarchical in structure. Accordingly, it was expected of the State that it should give absolute priority to the 'national' interest; more concretely, to the restoration of national sovereignty. This goal of liberation from all the constraints of the Treaty of Versailles was to take precedence over all other particular interests. Both the rapid changes of cabinet caused by changing parliamentary coalitions and the continual 'party squabbles', in the seclusion of the *Reichstag* and in the public at large, failed to meet these expectations. It was only logical that the *Reichswehr* officer corps in fact applied the same standard to right-wing elements as well, and frequently voiced strong disapproval of them.[48] Yet at the same time, there is no doubt that the officer corps as a whole, with what must be termed its reactionary concept of the function of the State, was a conservative, nationalist element in society and hence, doubtful in its loyalty to the Republic.

It is no surprise therefore that the *Reichswehr*'s and more particularly Groener's policy of co-operation, which necessarily implied the acceptance of compromises and the demands of coalition politics, found little sympathy in the officer corps. In contrast, they approved of Brüning's presidential system of government tolerated by parliament, which was founded on the authority of the Reich President and emergency decrees issued under article 48 of the constitution and which had, broadly speaking, relieved parliament of its capacity to influence and control.[49] The tide turned however when Brüning found himself forced to proceed with bans on radical right-wing movements.[50] The institutions of the Republic proved less and less able to withstand attacks from radicals on the right and left, and many leading officers, despite their aversion to the para-military organisations, believed that the 'national elements' which existed within the militant mass-movements should not be neglected. Consequently the rise of the National Socialist Party and the unrestrained aggression of the SA became a special problem for the *Reichswehr* with its marked national, conservative attitude. The idea of 'taming' the radical movement, expressed on numerous occasions by Groener and Schleicher,[51] did not meet with even temporary success. With the results of the elections[52] of April 1932 and subsequent events which led immediately to the fall of Brüning's presidential cabinet, the *Reichswehr*'s relationship with the Republic became even more strained. The Ministers of the Interior in the *Länder* and Groener as Reich Minister of the Interior regarded a ban on the SA as essential, and Brüning had authorised this.[53] But Schleicher opposed it, feeling that such a ban would undermine the policy of the *Reichswehr* which was designed to meet the needs of the Army rather than those of the Republican system.

Schleicher's premise was that a presidential régime, of the kind which had developed under Brüning since 1930, would have to rely all the more heavily on the confidence and support of the President, the less it could count on a mandate from parliament and public opinion. The elections of April 1932 had shown that there no longer existed a majority in favour of Brüning's policy and that the spring tide of National Socialist success had not yet ebbed. Groener's attempt, supported by Brüning and the *Länder* though not by

Hindenburg, to push through a comprehensive ban on the SA, worried Schleicher. He thought the *Reichswehr* could not afford to disagree with Hindenburg, given the close ties which existed between the *Reichswehr* and the office and person of the President. The growing distance between Hindenburg and Brüning since the end of 1931 and the conflict between Groener and the President which arose out of the SA ban touched a very sensitive nerve in the *Reichswehr*'s political self-estimation. Schleicher's break with Groener and his active participation in Brüning's fall were thus completely in line with military policy pursued up to that point.[54]

Groener's policy of co-operation with the executive of the Republic had secured the *Reichswehr* numerous advantages. The armaments programmes had brought the so-called 'post-Versailles era' closer, yet overall military policy remained within the bounds of the system of collective security under the League of Nations. The armaments programmes and the directive of April 1930 show Groener to have been a minister who applied himself energetically to his role as a military leader and who defined the 'Tasks of the *Wehrmacht*' with a broad political vision. In this he stands out among his predecessors and successors. He fell victim to the policy of co-operation which he himself had shaped and promoted but which had an increasingly narrow basis within and outside the executive. It was the Hitler–Blomberg 'alliance' which marked the decisive turning point for the *Reichswehr*.

2 Blomberg's Military Policy 1933/4

The appointment of General von Blomberg as Reich Defence Minister on 30 January 1933 took place under unusual circumstances. That he was sworn in before the assembled cabinet illustrates the significance which the circle around the Reich President and Papen attached to the *Reichswehr* as a stabilising factor in the first cabinet under National Socialist leadership. Even Hitler, who had originally wanted the office given to one of his Party colleagues, found Blomberg acceptable since he had already established what he regarded as satisfactory contact with him and with Reichenau, his Chief of Staff.

The co-operation which existed between Hitler and Blomberg was based on an arrangement which had a strong influence on future developments in domestic and foreign policy. In the first place it consisted of a renunciation of the *Reichswehr*'s former role of maintaining domestic order,[1] to which Blomberg agreed, and which the cabinet meeting of 30 January endorsed. Given a cabinet of 'national concentration' this renunciation was entirely in line with the *Reichswehr*'s own conception of its political role. From Hitler's point of view, Blomberg's support on this meant he could proceed with a radical reorganisation of the country's internal political affairs. In return, Hitler openly acknowledged the *Reichswehr* in its existing form as 'the most important institution in the State'. Above all, in order to achieve his political aims, Hitler, in the presence of the *Reichswehr* leadership, pledged himself to a comprehensive rearmament programme. Thus a consensus was reached on military–political goals which was to prove important in the following years in guaranteeing the stability of the régime. From the *Reichswehr*'s point of view, the 'alliance' meant, above all, that military and armaments objectives which they had been pursuing steadily for some time were guaranteed. The 'alliance' between Hitler and Blomberg, therefore, was based on an alignment of primary interests on both sides which ensured its strength and durability.[2]

The 'alliance' also had the effect of fundamentally altering the political function of rearmament. The change not only influenced the spheres of foreign and domestic policy but also had a radical effect on the scope and methods of armament itself, which in turn had a pronounced effect on the whole face of German politics. Blomberg and the *Reichswehr* played a very active part in this reorientation, the significance of which, in contrast to that of the political activities of Hitler and the National Socialist movement, has not up to now been fully recognised.

Although Hitler promised to promote armament by all possible means, the limitations imposed by Germany's external relations had still to be overcome. Blomberg, who had represented the *Reichswehr* in the German delegation at the disarmament conference in Geneva, was fully aware that as long as the Treaty of Versailles remained internationally binding, German rearmament was still to a great extent a problem of foreign policy. In their policies on national defence, Groener and Schleicher had taken account of this problem, which was further complicated by the Reich's geographic position in central Europe. The question was whether, with the change of government, a different emphasis would be placed on the evaluation of conditions imposed by the framework of external affairs.

Barely three weeks after Hitler's cabinet had taken charge of the affairs of government, the reaction to a French proposal made in Geneva showed clearly what priorities were being entertained within the German government on the necessity of securing a clear path to German rearmament.[3] The French Minister of Aviation, M. Cot, had submitted a plan for the standardisation of Europe's armies which was to solve the long-standing and controversial problem of security. The remarkable feature of this French initiative was its failure to provide concrete suggestions on a number of important questions. This seemed to provide some scope for negotiations, a fact which caused the leader of the German delegation in Geneva, Ambassador Nadolny, to speak of the conference having reached a turning point.

Even before a Foreign Office statement was issued, Blomberg left no doubt as to the new course envisaged for armaments policy. In a directive to the German delegation[4] he formulated a number of 'preliminary questions' which it was imperative to answer before discussing army standardisation. Among these preliminary questions the most controversial problems of disarmament were expressly pushed into the foreground, so that the Reich Defence Minister's intention to avoid any foreign control whatsoever on German armament became clearly discernible. The Foreign Secretary, von Neurath, who was convinced that German and French political goals were in every sense irreconcilable, endorsed Blomberg's view. Neither the possibility of a breakdown of the conference nor the increased isolation of the Reich seemed to deter the two Ministers. The level at which the decision was taken was characteristic: the Chancellor was not consulted. When in mid-March 1933 Freiherr von Rheinbaben, a member of the German delegation, in the presence of Neurath and Blomberg, reported to Hitler on the course of the conference, it became evident that Hitler had been intending to make use of the opportunities contained in the French proposal and had desired a 'positive outcome' for the conference, rather than 'armament outside the treaty'.[5] The Chancellor's instruction did not however prevent the Ministers from directing the German delegation to stick firmly to their own political guidelines.[6] These rather unorthodox procedures, so revealing for the initial phase of the National Socialist régime, show clearly how the 'alliance' with Hitler strengthened the Reich Defence Minister's position.

Hitler himself was convinced that the armament he so strongly supported was not, in the long run, compatible with *any* international armaments agreement, but that, in the first phase of 'rearming' (*Wiederwehrhaftmachung*) the German people, the risks of isolation or of sanctions, whether political or economic in nature, could be circumvented by skilfully applied political tactics. Because of this, in mid-May, Hitler overrode the views of his Foreign and Defence Ministers who had openly advocated Germany's withdrawal from the disarmament conference, choosing to avoid direct confrontation in favour of a policy of deception as outlined in his 'Peace Speech' of 17 May.[7] Up to the beginning of October[8] this strategy was followed. By that time, however, it had become clear that a British proposal to mediate, which was to be discussed at the conference in mid-October, would not improve Germany's armament status in the first phase of the agreement but on the contrary would introduce a system of armaments control. From this point on, Hitler himself decided to risk an open break with international institutions,[9] even though a few days before he had stated that it would be 'in any event desirable to bring about a disarmament agreement, even if it does not comply with all our wishes'. It would be wrong 'to demand more than we could obtain in the coming years, given the technical, financial and political means at our disposal'.[10] With the German government's declaration of 14 October 1933, and the withdrawal from both the League of Nations and the disarmament conference, German military and armament policies were finally extricated from the collective security system which had for so long been central in determining Germany's revisionist aims.

If at this juncture of political events one attempts to summarise developments in the sphere of national defence and the principles, from Groener to Blomberg, which lay behind them, the fundamental change is to be discerned in the factors determining national defence policy. Groener had defined it in terms of political categories and saw it as being defined by political factors, of which military potential was an important one, but which had to be integrated into the more general revisionist concept. His views on national defence found their best military expression in the April 1930 directive, 'The Tasks of the *Wehrmacht*'.[11] Groener's military and armament policies thus fell into line with the multilateral security system evolved after 1919. Although military goals remained unchanged, these ties were greatly loosened under Schleicher owing to pressures of domestic policy. Schleicher was the first to attempt a revision of the military conditions of the Versailles Treaty by means of bilateral negotiations.[12] However for Blomberg, the conditions governing foreign policy, accepted up to that time, no longer seemed binding for any German military and armaments policy. Earlier, as chief of the *Truppenamt*, he had already rejected Groener's concept of national defence and had adopted the position that it should be viewed solely from a military perspective.[13] After the experience of the First World War this was an astonishing narrowing of the military horizon which was to have serious consequences and which can be seen as a precondition for the 'alliance' between Hitler and Blomberg and for the long-term, essentially frictionless co-operation between the *Reichswehr* and the National Socialist régime. Groener's statement made in the directive of April 1930, to the effect that even the thought of a 'great War' could not be contemplated by the *Reichswehr* because of the totally unsatisfactory level of armament, was still valid. It was characteristic of the new direction of military policy that Blomberg belonged

to the group that expressly advocated unilateral German rearmament disregarding foreign policy considerations, even
though in the initial phase of rearmament the *Reichswehr* was
militarily weak, and that furthermore, he succeeded in implementing his views. In retrospect, the so-called 'Austrian corporal' saw the
limitations inherent in the Reich's foreign policy situation more
clearly than anyone. Blomberg's position on this question certainly
revealed, on the one hand, a professionalism which had been raised
to an ideology. On the other hand, however, it reflects the fact that
the 'rearming' of the nation had made great progress under
National Socialism and that popular support for armed strength
had greatly increased. In effect, the withdrawal of Germany from
the disarmament conference and the League of Nations, as
approved by Blomberg, marked the final departure from Groener's
policy of national defence, the main features of which had been its
incorporation of political factors and its basis in the collective
security system. The adventure of unrestricted rearmament had
begun.

At home the military leadership viewed their release from overall
political responsibility, through Hitler's appointment to the position of Reich Chancellor and Blomberg's take-over at the Reich
Defence Ministry, as a return to desired 'normalcy'.[14] As
Chancellor and Defence Minister, Schleicher had attempted to
enlarge the narrow basis of his own political activities by organising
particular sections of the population and social groups on a national
level.[15] All his steps in this direction depended upon the support of
the *Reichswehr* and its officer corps. A feverish political activity
developed at the Ministry under General von Bredow; men in the
confidence of Schleicher and the Defence Ministry held key
positions in the civil executive; and even the armed forces did not
remain unaffected by those political tasks, the direction of which
Schleicher had entrusted to the *Reichswehr*.[16] Yet even given this aid,
it still proved impossible for Schleicher to overcome the lack of
support his policies had in the various political and social groups. In
addition, the closely interlocking relationship between political and
military interests was increasingly criticised by the *Reichswehr*'s
officer corps. The criticism was not so much directed against
Schleicher's objectives in foreign and domestic policy, but rather at
the methods Schleicher was employing for their realisation, and in
particular the way in which the *Reichswehr* was increasingly being
used to carry out political tasks.[17] Thus on 30 January, Blomberg's

abandonment of the *Reichswehr's* function as upholder of political order at home was entirely in accord with the interests of the military leadership at that time.

On the other hand, Hitler's address to the *Reichswehr* generals on 3 February 1933, at the home of the Head of the Army Command, made clear the change in the basic situation affecting armed power and national defence in Germany.[18] Right at the outset Hitler announced that 'regaining political power' was to be his sole aim, and that this was dependent upon a complete 'volte face' of the existing domestic political circumstances and more especially on a 'strengthening of the will to arm' employing all possible means. Using several different dramatic examples, Hitler enlarged on his plans for 'rearming', promising that politically motivated opposition to the military organisation of national defence, against which the *Reichswehr* had been previously helpless, would be overcome. This programme for 'rearming' provided a firm basis for co-operation between the *Reichswehr* and the National Socialist movement represented by Hitler. For the first time the opportunity seemed to present itself for organising the German nation, with all its material and human resources, to meet the needs of the military and thus to create – in accordance with what were generally perceived as the lessons of the First World War – the decisive preconditions for an effective national defence. Hitler expressed this incisively when he said that success at the disarmament conference in Geneva would be 'pointless . . . if a nation [did not] possess the will to arm'. The fact that the *Reichswehr* was to be considerably more firmly anchored in the population, and that conscription would replace the small professional army, was of decisive importance in the view of the *Reichswehr* generals. An atmosphere of optimism became apparent. The dictum of early February 1933 of Colonel von Reichenau, the newly appointed Head of the Armed Forces Office, to the effect that the *Wehrmacht* had 'never before' been 'so identical with the State',[19] was wishful thinking in fact, but nevertheless described the exact goal it was intended to achieve.

At the same time intensive work went into the 'rearming' of the German people especially with regard to integrating the paramilitary forces into the scheme of national defence. The vehicle for this integration was the SA, the National Socialist paramilitary organisation, which was for a time indispensable to Hitler in domestic politics and was soon to prove indispensable to the military policies of the *Reichswehr* as well. This state of affairs, however, harboured specific dangers. In 1933 under Ernst Röhm the SA became numerically (partly due to the gradual integration of the *Stahlhelm*) and structurally the most powerful and tightly organised instrument of the régime.[20] It proved decisive that Röhm and the SA leadership wished to use this power for their own political and military purposes. This inevitably brought them into conflict with Hitler as well as with the *Reichswehr* leadership. The idea that the 'National Socialist revolution' had not yet achieved its ends and would only be able to surmount the last obstacles with the aid of the SA, the armed force of the revolution, had potential appeal, given that several million people were still unemployed in the autumn and winter of 1933 and given also the high ambitions nurtured by the functionaries in this mass movement.[21] In this respect the SA inevitably became a dangerous threat to Hitler, the Party leader and Reich Chancellor. But Hitler was successful in strengthening and consolidating his internal political position against Röhm by his withdrawal from the disarmament conference and the League of Nations, by the acceptance of his policies in the plebiscite and by the *Reichstag* elections of 12 November 1933 which were accompanied by the extensive use of propaganda.[22]

At times the *Reichswehr* was in an extremely exposed position vis-à-vis the SA. It had little with which to compete against the obvious assets of the SA: its confidence, the proximity of its leaders to the seat of power and its claim to be the Party's alternative to the Army. Certain shared ideological perspectives, the fluid boundaries between State, the Party and its armed wing and finally the military need to maintain the viability of the border defence units, all forced the *Reichswehr* to co-operate with the SA. Blomberg's and Reichenau's endeavours during the conflict with the SA were directed towards establishing the *Reichswehr* as the sole instrument of national defence and at convincing Hitler of its indispensability to the rearmament programme already under way. Thus they were prepared, for example, to dispense with the authoritative influence they could have exercised over pre-military training and the organisation of the Voluntary Labour Service.[23] The *Reichswehr* initially supported the SA in all questions of military training. This was made clear on 12 July 1933 when Hitler entrusted the SA with the task of training 250,000 SA officers and men within a year for possible use as *Reichswehr* auxiliary troops in the event of war.[24] This could only be done in co-operation with the *Reichswehr*, which dispatched special training units to SA training camps.[25] By lending assistance in training, however, the *Reichswehr* was giving indirect support to Röhm's intention to replace the *Reichswehr* with the SA at some future date. The extensive training obligations in the *Reichswehr*, in the border defence units and now also in the SA training camps, overburdened the capacities of the military machine almost beyond endurance. The training capacity of the *Reichswehr* was exhausted and this could only benefit the one organisation which placed the existence of the *Reichswehr* in question.[26] When Röhm advanced his claims more openly in October and November, adding actions to words,[27] it proved expedient for the *Reichswehr* to use all its energies for an extension of its own power base by exploiting every possibility for both material and personnel expansion.

Thus in autumn 1933, the *Reichswehr*'s armaments policy faced a new situation. Previous armament measures had been based on the planning of 1932, the goal of which had been to set up a 21-division field army by 1938. The material prerequisites for this had been created with the Second Armaments Programme[28] of early 1932 while the so-called 'Conversion Plan' (*Umbau-Plan*)[29] of November 1932 had prescribed the arrangements for increases in personnel for this period.

Hitler had been markedly reserved in his announcement of concrete armament measures to the *Reichswehr* generals at the beginning of February 1933. The reintroduction of general conscription was the only goal he regarded as self-evident, although he did not specify any date for it. Also Blomberg had warned the Commanders against nurturing 'exaggerated hopes and expectations'. The 'scope of what we wish and shall initially be able to build up' was, in his view, modest.[30] In the first place the possibilities were limited by the financial means at their disposal and – despite Blomberg's unorthodox view – on the appraisal at any one time of the extent of the Reich's room to manoeuvre in the sphere of foreign politics. Nevertheless in the early days of February 1933, a marked acceleration in the implementation of the Second Armaments Programme occurred as a result of additional funds being made available.[31]

Similar trends in the sphere of army personnel expansion were not to be expected since the creation of whole new units could scarcely have been concealed. For the year 1933, however, the Conversion Plan envisaged the removal of restrictive regulations governing the size of existing units, the creation of single units and in particular of artillery, anti-aircraft and signals units.[32] These measures were to increase army personnel strength by approximately 14,000. Contrary to the terms of the Treaty of Versailles, the new volunteers had to enlist for a period of three years. The recruitment of 85,000 men as short-term service supplementary troops had to be prepared for by organising the reserve services and establishing the relevant authorities. Alongside this considerable strengthening of the regular army, the Conversion Plan for 1933 included a second main task: to intensify the training of the border defence units. For this purpose nine border defence training batallions were to be formed which were intended to work in co-operation with the training divisions of the other sections of the Army to prepare the volunteer border defence units in two-week-long training courses.

The take-over of government by the National Socialists barely altered the basic features of this modest programme. Only the total of new enlistments seems to have been increased – by more than half again – over the number planned. In view of the threat represented by the development of the SA under Röhm, this relatively long-term armament planning no longer met the military and domestic political requirements of autumn 1933.

The general parameters of foreign policy had also altered in a manner beneficial to an accelerated process of German rearmament. After the withdrawal from the League of Nations and the disarmament conference, Hitler had declared to the British and French ambassadors his willingness to negotiate and reach a compromise.[33] He indicated possibilities for a solution, while at the centre of his offer lay the demand that Germany should be able to build up a 300,000-strong army with a one-year period of service without encountering any determined opposition and sanctions.

These foreign, domestic and military contingencies formed the background for the decision of December 1933 to create a 300,000-strong peacetime army.[34] In mid-December an unusual, not to say hectic development began in the Defence Ministry. A note added by the Head of the *Truppenamt*, General Ludwig Beck, to a memorandum from the Organisational Department of the *Truppenamt* on the 'Creation of the Future Peacetime Army', which had already been approved by the Minister, was dated 14 December. The Head of the *Truppenamt*'s basic directive on the creation of the new peacetime army followed only four days later, on 18 December. Finally, a Commanders' conference was convened for 20 and 21 December in Berlin, at which Blomberg, Beck and the other heads of departments explained the aims and details of planning. During the remaining days of December a great number of individual instructions were sent out in order to ensure that the implementation of the three-fold increase in the size of the Army could begin on 1 April 1934. There is no reliable information available regarding the particular reasons for this spate of extraordinary activity. It is highly probable however, that Blomberg and Reichenau were seeking to establish a fait accompli in their conflict with Röhm.

The *Reichswehr*'s new programme provided for the setting up of a peacetime army comprising 21 divisions over a period of four years i.e. between 1 April 1934 and 31 March 1938, and only dealt with the provision of personnel. The plans were based on the introduction of a one-year period of service, which would be replaced, according to the *Reichswehr* leadership, at the latest in the autumn of 1934 by compulsory military service. The three-fold increase in the Army was to be accomplished with the aid of reserve organisations already in existence. The military goal of the December programme is set out clearly in the memorandum of the Organisational Department. The peacetime army was to be the basis for the field army which was to be capable of 'conducting a defensive war on several fronts with a good chance of success'. The meaning of this statement only becomes evident when compared with earlier military objectives for the event of war as in Groener's 'Tasks of the *Wehrmacht*' and the 21-division field army. Was a defensive war on several fronts conceivable without the introduction of general conscription, without command of the industrial potential of the Ruhr and without military safeguards for the Rhine? These questions were not discussed in December 1933, but from previous *Reichswehr* planning, all the participating officers were aware of the fact that without an affirmative answer to these questions no defensive war against France was feasible. Only after these conditions were met could they count on the 63-division field army to complete its prescribed task. In this light Hitler's spectacular actions – the re-introduction of general conscription in March 1935 and the occupation of the Rhineland in 1936 – can be seen as having been programmed in advance in the military objectives and plans of 1933.

The extraordinary speed with which the programme was pushed through in the second half of December and with which the first steps towards its realisation were taken, indicates a political as well as a military motive. At the conference of Commanders in Berlin on 20 December, the Reich Defence Minister indirectly but clearly expressed motives of a domestic political nature which lay behind the programme. He explained that 'two major difficulties' had emerged 'on the question of defence': on the one hand, 'the organisation of the border defence units' and on the other, 'the efforts of the SA to establish an armed force in its own right'.[35] The *Reichswehr*'s December programme was intended as a counter measure to these problems. The training programme for volunteers had only begun in the spring of 1933 – volunteers who largely belonged to the SA – and was carried out within the framework of the border defence units in special training batallions. It was terminated on 31 March 1934 and the batallions were integrated into the peacetime army. At the same time the training commandos of the *Reichswehr* were to be recalled from the training camps of the SA. Because of the exceptional scarcity of officers, the *Reichswehr* leadership could no longer afford to waste its personnel. By concentrating on expanding its own sphere, the *Reichswehr* leadership had at the same time deprived its dangerous rival of crucial preconditions for its bid for military power.

Besides the foreign and domestic consequences of the December programme and the conditions it imposed, the aspect of armament also deserves attention. With the first phase of rearmament under National Socialist rule, the co-ordination between manpower and material planning achieved in 1932 had come adrift. The material resources of the 21-division peacetime army were provided for by the Second Armament Programme, but this left the 63-division field army with no comparable programme to secure it supplies and equipment.[36] The warning from the Chief of the Army Ordnance Office, that 'an Army which' had to 'throw down its weapons after *six* or *eight* weeks because of a total lack of ammunition or fuel' would be 'neither a useful instrument in the hands of a commander nor a power in the hands of the statesman', was not heeded. The discrepancy between the provision of manpower and material resources became one of the most characteristic problems of German rearmament after 1933.

Besides engaging in an active rearmament policy and consequently departing from the military provisions of the Treaty of Versailles, the new Reich Defence Minister also exercised a strong influence on the relationship between the armed forces on the one hand and the NSDAP, its affiliated organisations and the Nazi State on the other.

At the beginning of February 1933, Blomberg summarised future developments for the Commanders under three headings. He regarded it as his duty to use all available means to secure the position of the *Reichswehr* as a 'power which stands above-party', secondly to 'strengthen the *Wehrmacht* by mobilising the population' and thirdly to support 'the shaping of the *Wehrmacht* into a reliable instrument for maintaining national security'.[37] The key notion of the essentially above-party nature of the Army, which Blomberg quite consciously emphasised during the transition period in February 1933, not only restated a traditional political position but was also intended – in conjunction with his second point regarding the mobilisation of the population – to characterise the behaviour of the military leadership towards the new holders of political power. Adherence to the 'above-party principle' implied a clear distancing from the ruling NSDAP. If this position were abandoned, Blomberg believed that the *Reichswehr* would 'sink into the role of a Party Army' and that this would destroy the 'foundations upon which the *Reichswehr* had been built'.

This traditional and established political principle became difficult for the military leadership when, in the summer of 1933, it became evident that in the place of several political parties, a single party with totalitarian claims would determine the nation's politics. Remaining 'above-party' became not only conceptually but also politically impracticable in a one-party state. As early as March 1933, Blomberg abandoned the position he had adopted the month before and demanded that his military commanders give 'unquestioning support' to the 'national revolution'.[38] The Reich Defence Minister subsequently used every possible opportunity to point out that the NSDAP leaders deserved the full confidence of the *Reichswehr*, since the Party upheld the best national traditions of the past and acted in accordance with this heritage.[39] In 1933 Hitler's domestic and foreign policy decisions had supported Blomberg's arguments. Despite scepticism towards the Nazi Party and criticism of its political actions and methods, the officer corps, because the National Socialist movement's outlook on questions of internal order and foreign policy corresponded to a great extent with the living nationalist tradition in the *Reichswehr*, was unable to maintain the distance called for by its principle of standing 'above-party'. This 'partial identity of aims'[40] called for a new definition of the relationship between the *Wehrmacht* and the State.

In January 1934 Hitler himself, speaking on the anniversary of the '*Machtergreifung*' (seizure of power) found a useful formula in describing the nation and the State as 'supported by two pillars': politically by the '*Volksgemeinschaft* upheld by the National Socialist movement' and militarily 'by the *Wehrmacht*'.[41] This 'two pillar theory', in which Hitler declared the *Wehrmacht* to be the 'sole armed power (*Waffenträger*) in the Reich', corresponded fully to the view the *Reichswehr* leaders and the officer corps held of their own role. It implied a recognition of the autonomy of military power in the State and seemed to guarantee the decisive influence on the affairs of the State which the Military claimed. But the pillar image also expressed the competition which the *Wehrmacht* faced from the 'sole bearer of the nation's *political* will', namely the Party and its organisations. Since Hitler was not only the Head of State, but at the same time the uncontested leader of a totalitarian political party, the time was not far away when the armed forces would no longer be viewed as a part of the foundations of the State, but simply as an instrument of power and therefore divested of the autonomy and influence which lay at the base of the 'two pillar theory'. That point was reached in 1938 after which there existed a 'National Socialist *Wehrmacht*' with Adolf Hitler as its Commander-in-Chief.

The political history of the *Wehrmacht* in the years 1933–9 is usually viewed against the background of the important political role that the *Reichswehr* had played in the Weimar Republic. It should not however be overlooked, that specific political preconditions which allowed the *Reichswehr* to develop into an important factor in domestic politics more or less disappeared after 1933. More important, in the course of two years the military command and the officer corps were freed from all foreign and domestic restrictions, which before January 1933 had hindered the fulfilment of their military objectives. Complete concentration upon the rapidly expanding military tasks not only decreased political activity within the *Wehrmacht* but also diminished its importance as a factor in domestic politics.

In January 1934 when Hitler formulated the 'two pillar theory', the *Reichswehr* still carried political weight in domestic affairs. Indeed this was crucial for the internal stability of the régime, because Röhm's SA threatened not only the position of the *Reichswehr*, but was potentially dangerous for the Party as well. Developments from the so-called *Machtergreifung* up to the Röhm purge at the end of June and beginning of July 1934 seemed from the *Reichswehr*'s point of view to confirm the good judgement and success of the political line taken by Blomberg and more especially by Reichenau. The ideological adjustment to the new régime, which had really asked very little of the officer corps with its strongly nationalistic and militaristic traditions and views, had been rewarded by the elimination of their most dangerous rival in the right to exercise armed power.

In his speeches and articles, Blomberg advocated that the *Reichswehr* should become more 'open' in its relations with the National Socialist régime[42] and right from the beginning he initiated appropriate measures, which ranged from permission given to the Army Music Corps to play National Socialist anthems (*Weihelieder*) to the *Reichswehr*'s adoption of the Aryan paragraph.[43] There followed the active participation in the elimination of Röhm and his SA, acquiescence to the murder of Generals von Schleicher and von Bredow,[44] the steady intensification of 'national political instruction courses' at all levels and, above all, the *Wehrmacht*'s oath of allegiance to Adolf Hitler as taken immediately, on the initiative of Blomberg and Reichenau, on the day of Hindenburg's death.[45] All this meant that the 'adaptation' and 'opening' of the *Wehrmacht* amounted to a process of almost complete ideological assimilation into the National Socialist régime. Blomberg continued this co-ordination with National Socialist *Weltanschauung*[46] until his dismissal at the end of January 1938. Neither recurrent conflicts with various groups within the Party nor the breakdown of the Army's monopoly of armed power through Hitler's creation of three armed SS regiments[47] prevented him from pursuing this course.

Blomberg and his Chief-of-Staff Reichenau proceeded from the assumption, based on the lessons of the First World War, that the rearmament of the *Wehrmacht* could only be conceived and realised if in peacetime a thorough restructuring of the nation for the eventuality of war could be organised and controlled by the military leadership. These conditions moreover could only be realised if the *Wehrmacht* were firmly anchored in the State and its people. Only then could the military leadership exercise the full measure of influence appropriate to its responsibility for the nation in times of conflict. This concept broke down very early on, when the three branches of the *Wehrmacht* failed to subordinate themselves to the *Wehrmacht* leadership on important issues.[48] The same could be said of important sections of the State Executive. Blomberg's influence on Hitler is difficult to assess in detail. His importance was undoubtedly diminished by the progressive stabilisation of the régime and by the increased importance for rearmament of economic factors. In autumn 1935 Reichenau, who was more keenly aware than Blomberg of the *Wehrmacht*'s political interests and who protected these against the Party and its organisations with greater tactical awareness was replaced by Keitel. This change also contributed to the fact that the *Wehrmacht*'s integration into the National Socialist State precluded it from exercising as decisive an influence as had originally been intended.

The political manoeuvring of the *Wehrmacht* leadership was viewed critically by the Army, Navy and Air Force commands. On the whole, this critical attitude was less dissatisfied with the general direction of Blomberg's political line than with the methods of its implementation, which were rejected. Even Hitler took the view that Blomberg often tried a little too hard to force the *Wehrmacht* to make political adjustments.[49] Despite all this – even after the elimination of the SA – tensions between the *Wehrmacht* and the National Socialist agencies submerged only to resurface in the Blomberg and Fritsch crisis of 1938. This was because for Hitler, it was more important to place the Military and its power unquestionably at the disposal of his expansionist policies than to achieve its ideological assimilation (*Gleichschaltung*). And on this score, despite all Blomberg's efforts, Hitler continued to distrust the higher officer corps which had been schooled in the *Reichswehr*.

3 The Army Armament Programme of August 1936

During discussions held in December 1933 Blomberg, the Reich Defence Minister, had attached great importance to the statement that armaments planning for the next four years was not to be considered an 'improvisation'. Thus he gave the gathered *Reichswehr* officers present the impression, just as the head of the *Truppenamt*, General Ludwig Beck had done, that rearmament would be carried out in gradual stages within the framework of this planning.[1] A few months later, however, it became clear that the *Reichswehr* leadership was unable to keep to its intentions for reasons of foreign and above all military policy.

In the sphere of foreign policy, Hitler's efforts to conceal the initiation of rearmament (which on the whole had been very successful) suffered a considerable set-back as a result of the French note of 17 April 1934.[2] The French government had effectively countered Hitler's tactic of diplomatic concealment by breaking off Franco-German discussions on an armaments agreement. The international risks generated by unilateral German armament became more and more acute. As a result, in May 1934, Hitler called for the final setting up of the planned 300,000 strong army for October of that year. The *Reichswehr* leadership did succeed in deferring this date by one year but from this point on, at the latest, one is no longer justified in speaking of a well-planned, long-term programme of armament.[3] As early as February 1935 the Army had reached a strength of 280,000 men!

Besides Hitler's repeated demands over the years, which were very general in nature in calling for a considerable acceleration of the process of armament, the 'improvisations' were also a result of the military leadership's own objectives. Blomberg's view, based on pre-First World War concepts, that the security of a state in the face of external danger could be achieved by military means[4] had met with the broad agreement of the Army leadership and the *Truppenamt* and had been reflected, for example, in the armament programme of December 1933. The aim of this programme was to build up an army which should be capable of waging a war on several fronts with 'a good chance of success'. This was a goal which could not be achieved through a volunteer army. The increase of army personnel in 1933–4 had resulted from the recruitment of volunteers enlisted for varying periods of service.[5] The military leadership, however, had always considered this form of recruitment as an unsatisfactory interim solution. Impressed by the need to speed up the creation of the 300,000-man army they began to regard the introduction of general conscription (in December 1933 Beck had already demanded it for autumn 1934[6]) as an urgent necessity. The proclamation of military sovereignty[7] on 16 March 1935, and the introduction of general conscription with a one-year period of service, effective from 1 October 1935, was not, therefore, a surprise tactic on Hitler's part but the fulfilment of a promise made to the generals in early February 1933 which had become politically feasible following the return of the Saar to the Reich.

Similarly one can be sceptical of reports suggesting that the armament target announced on 16 March of a peacetime army of 36 divisions had actually been conceived by Hitler himself.[8] Indeed, this announcement corresponded to a large extent with military planning. Once again this can be traced back to the objective of the programme of December 1933 to create a field army that 'would be capable of entering into a defensive war on several fronts with a good chance of success'. In 1934 the *Truppenamt* made several attempts to give this very general requirement and the conditions governing its implementation a tangible form. In view of an assumed coalition against the Reich, consisting of France, Belgium, Poland and Czechoslovakia, it was important that the geographical situation east of the Rhine, and the fear of the high mobility of the French army, meant that a relatively high number of operational divisions (9 to 10) would have to be available to counter any attack launched by France. These divisions would thus not be available as cadres for the field formations which were to be set up. A *Truppenamt* study of 6 March 1935 which was approved by the Chief of the Army Command, called for the formation of a peacetime army of 30 to 36 divisions.[9] Compared with the planning of December 1933, however, the figure for the required field army divisions remained practically unchanged at 63 to 73. There was thus a striking conformity between the armament target announced by Hitler and that of the military planners. The only point of controversy between the political and military leadership was the date by which the joint armament objective should be completed. Hitler demanded completion by autumn 1935. Within the Army Command voices were raised which wanted at least to have the organisational framework for the size and scope of the future army by this date. Fritsch and Beck, however, succeeded in moderating the speed at which the army was built up, in view of the probable adverse effect undue haste would have had on its operational readiness although even they revised their initial ideas after a relatively short period. They already had 36 infantry and 3 armoured divisions at their disposal by autumn 1936,[10] whereas they had initially envisaged reaching this target by autumn 1939.

The Rhineland crisis of March 1936 must also be viewed against the background of armaments policy. In considering the formation of an army of 36 divisions, difficulties regarding defence against France came to light which arose from the existence of the demilitarised zone. The timely acquisition of the Rhine in the event of a conflict was considered the sine qua non for a successful defence effort – even if only a temporary one. Since the mid-twenties, efforts had therefore been made within the *Truppenamt* to form a paramilitary defence organisation in the western border areas which had been intended at least to delay any French advance.[11] After initiatives of this kind had been blocked by Groener and Schleicher for reasons of foreign policy in the period from 1929 to 1933, Blomberg in his capacity as Defence Minister repeatedly insisted, against the wishes of the Foreign Office,[12] on the setting up of a strengthened border surveillance service. This service was organised with the support of civil administrative agencies making use of regional police forces stationed in the area as well as paramilitary units. Although it was difficult to evaluate the military efficiency of the surveillance service, accurate computations could be made which indicated the speed with which the regular units stationed east of the demilitarised zone could be moved to the Rhine. In February 1936 the responsible section of the General Staff, as the *Truppenamt* was known after summer 1935, concluded that transportation movements could not be effected in the time available.[13] Thus the demilitarised zone constituted an almost insuperable obstacle to attaining the strategic objectives that had been postulated as early as December 1933.

This obstacle assumed even more dangerous dimensions given the shape of the armament economy. At the end of the twenties and in the early thirties, the *Reichswehr* leadership had made efforts to sponsor important production branches located right in the geographic centre of the Reich or to shift to these areas. In view of the traditional significance of the Ruhr area for the production of weapons and equipment these measures met with relatively little success.[14] In the event of the mobilisation of 63 to 70 divisions, planned for an emergency, the Ruhr would be of crucial importance in securing supply services. Since the appearance of the above General Staff study, at the latest, it was clear that the extension of the Reich's military sovereignty to include the demilitarised zone was an indispensable military requirement to safeguard the growth of power already achieved and to provide a reliable production base for the armament programme. When Hitler decided to occupy the demilitarised zone, on 7 March 1936, he was certainly not influenced in his choice of date by his obvious awareness of the military situation. It may be assumed that a favourable situation in the sphere of foreign policy[15] and possibly also general political motives at home – as suggested by the subsequent Reichstag elections – contributed to this decision. Yet the action was a logical step on the way to 'regaining political power' since the operational capacity of the armed forces, according to Hitler indispensable to his political objectives, was decisively improved by the occupation of the demilitarised zone. The original scope of the armament programme of December 1933 was thus fundamentally altered by the above military considerations and by Hitler's general demands that its implementation be speeded up.

The proclamation of 16 March 1935 had set out new data for army armament, with the result that in early summer 1935 the offices of the Army High Command (*Oberkommando des Heeres,* previously *Heeresleitung*) were again already working on long-term plans for the build-up of a peacetime army of 36 divisions and its concomitant problems. As a result of this in part controversial debate the General Staff submitted a plan in mid-July which envisaged the setting up of an army of approximately 700,000 men by the beginning of October 1939.[16] Although Fritsch, the Army's Commander-in-Chief, gave his approval to the programme, Blomberg, Commander-in-Chief of the Armed Forces, refused to endorse it. It is not clear from the available sources what led him to make this decision. It is very probable, however, that Blomberg wished to await Hitler's decision, based on his military policy, on the re-establishment of military sovereignty in the Rhineland before bringing any long-term plans for army expansion into force.

The plans made in summer 1935 met with opposition in the Army High Command in the person of General von Schwedler, Head of the Army Personnel Office, although his criticisms were not heeded. The controversy is worth mentioning because it clearly shows how far the speed and extent of armament altered the structure of the Army even at this early date. Schwedler completely rejected 'any significant increase in the size of the Army planned for 1936' because at this time – in June 1935 – it was already no longer the case that there was 'an officer corps in the true sense'.[17] The quality and homogeneity of the officer corps had been considerably reduced by the inclusion of older, inactive officers, of police officers, and by falling back on reliable non-commissioned officers. Yet even these unusual measures could not meet the rapidly growing need.

In December 1933 Beck, Chief of the General Staff, had proceeded on the basis that the officer corps would form 7 per cent of the future army. He did however regard a figure of 3 per cent as satisfactory for the first phase of the build-up.[18] In October 1935 the proportion of active officers was still only 1·7 per cent although the addition of the so-called 'E-Officer Corps' brought the percentage up to 2·4.[19] The significance of the problem mentioned by Schwedler under the heading 'Quality and Quantity' can only be appreciated by a comparison with the conditions set by Seeckt and valid till 1932/3 regulating the selection and training of *Reichswehr* officers. All leading officers in the *Reichswehr* and the *Wehrmacht* and Fritsch and Blomberg in particular were deeply committed to these.[20] Yet Beck himself in summer 1935 saw no reason to give way to Schwedler's suggestions. Hitler's desire to hold to the quickest possible build-up by organising the 36-divisions field army according to mobilisation procedures and Beck's own diagnosis of the 'instability of political relations within Europe' were decisive in his decision to carry out a build-up of the Army 'as speedily and as uninterruptedly as possible'. In his view a reduction in the speed or scope of armament was out of the question.[21] Under the dictates of his own military aims and influenced by an appreciation of foreign affairs, which was in turn also coloured by those aims, the Chief of the General Staff pressed for a continuation of a forced rearmament. He did this even at the risk of impairing the efficiency of the officers brought together in the officer corps, the most important functional element in the military hierarchy.

It was not however the extremely precarious situation of the officer corps and the question of officer recruitment which occupied the Army High Command and the General Staff over the winter period of 1935–6, but the debate on 'Increasing the Army's Offensive Capacity'. This must be seen in conjunction with the setting up on 15 October 1935 of the first three armoured divisions.[22] The discussions could have had a considerable effect on the structure of the Army and this is, therefore, conceivably another reason why Blomberg rejected any binding decisions on the armament programme in 1935. With the order to set up the three armoured divisions, the development had reached an interim conclusion which provides an excellent example of how the Treaty of Versailles affected the thoughts and actions of the German military leadership. The terms of the treaty forced the *Reichswehr* leadership to tackle the problem of how to achieve the greatest possible military effect at the smallest possible cost, in terms of material and personnel. This led to the demand for a high level of mobility since quick success only seemed possible if surprise tactics were used. However the mobility of their own forces, intended to surprise the enemy, was only conceivable if motorised vehicles were used alongside rail transport. Two things emerged from this: a motorisation programme[23] and the idea of an independent, operative armoured division which Guderian had been championing since 1929. In Germany Guderian's name stood for a small group of officers during the late twenties and early thirties who were inspired by an intensive preoccupation with the problem of road transport movements and had developed forms of conducting combat using mechanised units.[24] Despite varied and frequent opposition, the organisational form of a modern, technologically advanced combat division, as recommended by these officers, won through in summer 1935. In July of that year at a demonstration of new weapons, Guderian had the opportunity of showing Hitler some of the motorised elements brought together in an armoured division. Hitler seemed very impressed and in the presence of the Commander-in-Chief of the Army emphatically welcomed Guderian's new concept. A month later a 'Test armoured Division' went on four-week manoeuvres. The aim was to demonstrate the possibilities for commanding large, highly mobile armoured units in combat and in conjunction with ancillary forces. The course of this exercise was also applauded by the Army's Commander-in-Chief[25] and the successful demonstration had a decisive effect on the further development of the Army.

The next main question which came to the fore in discussions was how to organise an effective defence against the demoralising attack of such armoured divisions. Fritsch had spoken in favour of an 'offensively conducted defence'[26] and this became and remained the principle behind all subsequent General Staff considerations. The idea of 'mobility in combat', of delaying actions, had been a necessity from the outset in view of the limitations of their own resources of power. From this point on the possibilities for conducting 'mobile fighting' were to increase considerably. With the notion of an 'offensively conducted defence' offensive out-flanking movements had become a real possibility.

The debate reached a high point with a memorandum from Beck to the Commander-in-Chief of the Army of 30 December 1935, which set out the direction and criteria for the whole discussion.[27] Entitled 'Considerations on Increasing the Offensive Capacity of the Army', it denied that the intended increased offensive capacity meant another scheme for increasing the size of the Army. The intention stated previously in the programme of December 1933 – namely of being able with the use of the mobilised field army to wage a war on several fronts with a good chance of success – still obtained. Beck did add, however, that 'strategic defence . . . [would] only be successful if it were able to be carried out in the form of an attack'. The concept of 'strategic defence' shows how a new interpretation had been imposed on the objectives of 1933 as a result of a change in circumstances. The General Staff of the Army now took the liberty of thinking 'on a larger scale'. Its concepts were now very close to the Moltke and Schlieffen tradition, whose strategical concept of a war on several fronts could also be characterised as an offensively conducted defence.

Besides the three armoured brigades of the three armoured divisions, planning had up to this point provided for a further three brigades to work with the troops. Meanwhile Beck held the view that it was both necessary and realistic that each corps of the peacetime army should be assigned one armoured brigade. This amounted to doubling the number of armoured brigades already planned.

More important than this increase in numerical strength, however, was the use to which Beck wished to see the armoured divisions put. He saw it as a matter of three main tasks: 1. to support the infantry ('Inf. Tank'), 2. armoured defence and 3. their 'independent operative use in association with other motorised weapons (at present armoured divisions)'. Beck devoted a separate study to the third of these. A frontal attack against an enemy equal in strength and numbers could 'hardly expect to succeed' unless supported by tanks. Beck also made the point that 'long-range targets' could only be envisaged if armoured divisions were brought into play and that, consequently, the composition of the existing armoured divisions should be examined. The general impression given by the memorandum is that Beck differed only slightly from Guderian on the use of tank formation,[28] although the Chief of the General Staff favoured greater flexibility in questions of organisation.

Consequently Beck's plans amounted to a radical restructuring of the Army. Although he kept within the guidelines of the 36-division army envisaged in summer 1935, the military leadership was now nevertheless to have motorised and mechanised combat units for long-range target attacks at its disposal by the end of the 1939/40 build-up phase. In an emergency these units were to constitute more than a third of the peacetime divisions. This created totally different military conditions for 'strategic defence' in a war on several fronts. The German Army had already well overtaken the armies of its neighbours by the setting up of three armoured divisions and Beck's programme would again increase this advantage considerably.

The result of this debate still remained to be converted into a concrete, comprehensive and realisable armament plan. The Chief of the General Staff, however, had already let it be known that neither financial nor economic difficulties would prevent him pursuing the recognised and correct military aim. When the Chief of the General Army Office expressed doubts as to whether the demands for 12 armoured brigades were financially feasible, Beck totally rejected the notion of a reduction 'for financial reasons'.[29] In a comment on the equipping and organisation of the projected armoured divisions he demanded that they should be freed 'from the present, still limited possibilities with regard to armament'. It was, rather, to be 'the targets set by the leadership for the combat units' which were to take precedence in deciding the final aim to be achieved.[30] This disdain for the basic economic principles which must be observed if a modern army is to be planned effectively shows once again how vain was the attempt in May 1934 by the Head of the Army Ordnance Office to point out to the military leadership the equal importance of material and personnel factors for rearmament and to get them to take adequate account of realistic 'possibilities with regard to armament' when making their plans.[31]

Two years after the decision to build up a 21-division army, the rearmament process had reached a new stage with the 'Considerations on Increasing the Offensive Capacity of the Army'. This development came at a time when overall army planning was stagnating, when the urgent decision on the activation phase of autumn 1936 had yet to be taken and the extension of military sovereignty to include the demilitarised zone was regarded as purely a matter of time. Nor could the conventional type of division – even taking its present stage of development into account – be judged up to standard. The build-up of a field army as planned was still in its very early stages. This open situation made it easy to integrate solutions to the organisational and operational problems connected with the tank forces into the planning of the overall structure of the future army. This new army became a concrete possibility following the reoccupation of the Rhineland in March 1936. Hitler's political success together with the consequences of military considerations on 'Increasing the Offensive Capacity of the Army' led once again to a further speeding up and extension of the dynamic process of rearmament.

As early as January 1936 there had been new developments in the Army General Staff's ideas on the subject of the new units to be set up in autumn 1936 which now went far beyond the planning dates set in summer 1935.[32] These also had been out-dated by the occupation of the Rhineland. Up to this point it had been assumed that the total of 36 divisions mentioned by Hitler on 16 March 1935 also included the armoured divisions. But now as stated in an Activation Order of 1 April, the Army was to consist of 36 infantry divisions, 3 armoured divisions, 1 mountain division and 1 cavalry brigade – a total of 41 divisions.[33] The number of infantry divisions rose from 24 to 36, a 50 per cent increase on the total set up in autumn 1935. All in all the Army had reached a strength of about 520,000 men by the autumn of 1936.

Thus the medium-term build-up planning of summer 1935 had gone completely off the rails, although since then the political situation itself had completely changed. In addition the 'Considerations on Increasing the Offensive Capacity of the Army' meant that the pre-conditions had been created for a further expansion of the Army. These conditions were to form the basis for detailed planning and made possible urgently required long-term measures. On 8 June 1936 the Commander-in-Chief of the Army,

Colonel-General von Fritsch, held a conference. Although no report is available on the conference proceedings or on its concrete results, it nevertheless set out particular priorities and charged the General Staff with the responsibility for detailed planning.

Only a few days later on 12 June the Chief of the General Staff submitted concrete data on the strength of the future peacetime and field army as well as on specific measures to be taken during the coming years. According to these figures the peacetime army was eventually to comprise:[34] 36 infantry divisions of which 4 were to be motorised, 3 armoured divisions, 3 light divisions, 1 mountain division and 1 cavalry brigade. According to General Staff calculations, the overall strength of the army was to be 793,410, of which 33,943 were to be officers. For the mobilisation year 1940–1 during which the formation of the field army was also to have been more or less completed, planning figures for the field army provided for 72 infantry, 3 armoured, 3 light and 21 reserve divisions as well as 7 armoured, 1 cavalry and 2 mountain brigades. As from October 1940, the personnel strength was to be 3,612,673, including reserves. Although Beck did not mention it explicitly, the plan reveals that the formation of the peacetime and field armies was to be completed by autumn 1939. But he did point out that the project depended essentially on 'the provision of necessary materials, including an adequate quantity of supplies and provisions', an argument he had flatly rejected a few months before.

Compared with the programme of December 1933 and the planning of summer 1935, these data, particularly as far as the field army was concerned, seemed at first sight to be contained within strict limits. With 72 infantry divisions, the upper limit that Beck had thought necessary as early as March 1935 had been reached. The most important difference was that an additional 21 reserve divisions were available and that the army and corps troops had been considerably enlarged so that the planned field army comprised 102 divisions in all. The German army in the field in 1914 had consisted of 87 divisions and 44 reserve brigades; the German wartime strength in 1914 amounting to 2,147,000 men was less than that projected for October 1940! Was it only due to political pressure exerted by Hitler after the occupation of the Rhineland that the military were compelled within the space of little more than seven years to exceed by far the results which the Imperial Army had required more than forty years of development to bring about?

The problems concealed behind these target figures can be

inferred from the projected increase in the size of the officer corps. According to a memorandum of 24 July 1936 from the Organisational to the Central Department of the General Staff, the necessary strength of the officer corps of the peacetime army in 1941 had been envisaged at approximately 33,950, although calculations showed that its actual strength would in fact be more in the region of 20,800,[35] and this given that there were no resignations and that the 'natural retirement' of officers was kept to a minimum. The shortfall of 13,150 officers could not under normal circumstances have been made good before 1950! In 1936 the proportion of officers including E-officers to the entire personnel strength of the Army was 2·6 per cent; without E-officers just 1·6 per cent![36] In 1941 the proportion including E-officers was to remain at the 1936 level. As in 1935, however, Beck seemed to be prepared to put up with these circumstances because – while referring to the example of the Imperial Army of 1914 which of course had no relevance at all in this context – he stated that 'peace and wartime personnel requirements' would only 'then be filled to a more or less acceptable level' when '3/5 of overall strength was available in the *regular* army'.[37] This corresponded roughly to the planned ratio of 2·6 per cent. Although the general qualitative deterioration which would increase as a result of the proposed measures was evident, 'present necessity' – as it was termed in a communication from the Organisational Department – left no other choice. What did this 'present necessity' mean to the Chief of the General Staff, burdened by responsibility for a development which contradicted his principles as a military expert? As before, his judgement on the state of foreign affairs was full of scepticism[38] and he was also aware that the isolation of the Reich could be traced back above all to the character and activities of National Socialist policies. Nevertheless he closed his eyes to the effects of armament on foreign affairs and hence succumbed to the circular argument that the threat manifested as a result of isolation could only be met by further accelerating armament efforts. In addition it is conceivable that the Chief of the General Staff might not have been unaffected by a fascination with the possibilities that armament opened up, a fascination which arose from the task of conducting a 'strategic defence' in the event of a European war on several fronts.

On the basis of a directive issued by the Commander-in-Chief of the Army, the General Army Office in co-operation with other agencies of the High Command began detailed planning on the basis of data submitted by the General Staff. On 1 August 1936 Major General Fromm was able to provide the Commander-in-Chief with impressive statistics.[39] His presentation shows much more distinctly than the General Staff plan of 12 June that the Commander-in-Chief of the Army was working to establish the operational readiness, not only of the peacetime, but also of the field army by 1 October 1939. Fromm pointed out that this requirement faced 'serious difficulties regarding the supply of tanks and ammunition, truck mobilisation requirements and the unpredictable areas of raw materials, machinery and skilled workers'. He nevertheless arrived at the conclusion that 'the activation and supply of the required army during peace and war-time . . . could be guaranteed on a purely *theoretical level*', provided the required funds and foreign exchange would be made available 'in time'. However it was doubtful whether this requirement would be fulfilled. The total funds necessary for the planned measures for 1937–45 were calculated[40] as shown in Table 3.1.

TABLE 3.1

Financial year	Previous financial requirements (Summer Plan 1935)	New financial requirements*
1937	3575	8882
1938	3675	8979
1939	3859	8858
1940	3439	4669
1941	2584	4294
1942	2584	3499
1943	2584	3469
1944	2584	3469
1945	2584	3169

* Figures in thousand million Reichsmarks.

From the figures for nine financial years one can clearly discern the dimensions of the High Command's August programme. Financial requirements rose to almost double those of the summer 1935 plan and this had already scheduled a doubling of the 300,000 strong army of the 1933 December programme. Further Fromm's report did not mention the expenditure which would result from the military demand for constant readiness for war. In order to meet this demand, 'the mobilisation capacity of the armaments industry' would have to be sustained 'by continuous, large minimum purchase orders from 1940 onwards even though such a large requirement *did not exist*'. According to the calculations of the Army Ordnance Office *these* costs would from 1942 onwards amount to more than was to be spent on the upkeep of the peacetime army. (see Table 3.2.)

TABLE 3.2

Financial year	Financial requirement*	Cost of minimum orders	Total
1940	4669	2900	7569
1941	4294	3325	7619
1942	3499	3750	7249
1943	3469	4175	7644
1944	3469	4600	8069
1945	3169	4600	7769

* Figures in thousand million Reichsmarks.

These figures implied facts which must have appeared very unreasonable even to the military planners. To take one example, from 1940 onwards as a result of minimum procurement rates, an annual increase of 36,000 machine guns had to be taken into account which could not be made use of.[41] Examples taken from the field of ammunition production reveal even more drastically that unacceptable conditions threatened to arise from the military's point of view, purely for the sake of maintaining operational readiness, the necessity of which had neither been explained nor questioned by Beck or Fromm.

These facts and figures led the military commanders, that is Blomberg, Fritsch, Beck and other leading officers of the High Command, to consider the rationale of their activities. Armament planning had arrived at a crucial point. In a memorandum to his Commander-in-Chief, Major General Fromm had unequivocally formulated the central question arising from the programme as follows: 'In the aftermath of the armament period the *Wehrmacht* must soon be employed in action or the pace be slackened by reducing requirements for the level of operational readiness'. Before a final recommendation could be made, Fritsch would as suggested by Fromm have to find out from the Reich Defence Minister what the situation was regarding foreign exchange and raw materials as well as the possibility of launching a large-scale export drive as of 1940. The latter would be designed to reduce the burdens caused by the minimum procurement rates. But above all it was necessary to determine whether or not there was 'any firm intention of employing the *Wehrmacht* at a date already fixed'.

To these all-important questions Fromm received no definite answer. Instead the decisions taken in the second half of 1936 left no doubt that from this time onwards army armament was carried out in accordance with the original August programme.

What political ends were served by this forced rearmament activity? A survey of the development of armament efforts from 1933 onwards leads to the conclusion that the August programme was only a further stage in a dynamic process which was primarily accelerated by military factors. It should also be borne in mind that the political objectives of armament planning were consonant with the programme explained by Hitler to the *Reichswehr* generals at the beginning of February 1933. Its substance was taken by the military commanders to mean the restoration of the Reich's position as a major European power, an objective that had been an aim of the *Reichswehr* leadership ever since 1919. The economic consequences of rearmament, the enormous and chronic financial burden involved and the possible social consequences were only of very minor importance in the eyes of the military commanders. Besides this element of continuity however the August programme shows the decisive change-over from a defensive rearmament to one explicitly offensive in direction. With this armament planning, the way had already been charted out for the possible change of course to a war of aggression by the turn of the year 1939/40. In early February 1934 Blomberg had stated that it was not Hitler's intention 'to attack anybody at all upon completion of rearmament'[42] but this was somewhat modified by the August programme. From now on those responsible for armament planning thought in terms of military aggression.

On 12 October 1936 Fritsch submitted the plan of the Army High Command to Blomberg[43] which began with the sentence: 'According to the Führer, a powerful army is to be created within the shortest possible time'. If this general wording was a true reflection of Hitler's instructions, then it was the military commanders who had given definite form to his ideas on a possible schedule. Fritsch asserted that the Army High Command was 'well able to cope with the bulk of this task by 1 October 1939'. Inquiries had revealed that a peacetime army comprising 830,000 men and a field army of 4,626,000 men could be in service by this date. The last figure far exceeded the data provided by Beck in June.

The principal questions raised by Fromm were only superficially dealt with in a communication from the Commander-in-Chief of the Army. An awareness of the dependence of military planning on political and economic factors is evident only in a few places. For example Fritsch contemplating the 'fuel and rubber situation' stated that supplies seemed 'assured if the economy were slowed down to some extent which was now a certainty following the implementation of the Führer's Four-Year Plan'. At a very early stage the military commanders replaced objective discussions with political credos. Blomberg was made responsible for materials and foreign exchange since this constituted the 'innate sphere of competence' of the War economy Staff which was directly sub-ordinate to the Reich Defence Minister.[44] The Commander-in-Chief of the Army commented on the crucial question of minimum procurement rates as follows: 'The large industrial capacity which will then be achieved [from 1940 onwards] strictly speaking requires the spending of considerable funds for further procurement orders although *Wehrmacht* requirements are in fact negligible. It is obviously not feasible to cope with these difficulties in this way. Other ways and means must be found urgently'.

Certainly there are few pieces of evidence which reveal in such clarity the unwillingness of the military leadership to face up to the consequence of their actions on behalf of the military apparatus for which they were responsible. In the final analysis Fritsch had but one objective: to carry out the task set for him in the manner described above. He evaded the consequences although they touched upon his area of competence by simply disclaiming them. At the beginning of December 1936 he declared the armament plan to be '*the basis for all further measures*' and authorised the Army Ordnance Office to place long-term supply contracts with the industry on the respective total requirements for weapons, equip-ment and ammunition which were computed under the overall plan.[45]

With the decision of the Commander-in-Chief of the Army of 6 December 1936 the last comprehensive armament plan before the outbreak of war had been implemented. After the armament programmes of December 1933, summer 1935 and spring 1936, i.e. after the full restoration of military sovereignty manifested in the occupation of the Rhineland, the move towards an army capable of conducting offensive operations had been taken. As regards quality, one looked to the results of an intensive debate on 'Increasing Offensive Capacity' which took into account solely military criteria. Another feature of planning was the short-term deadline. During a period of scarcely three years not only the peacetime army (which in October 1936 had been increased as far as units were concerned by nearly 50 per cent) but also an enormous field army, which up to this point had hardly made an appearance, were to be brought up to strength and fully equipped. The time-schedule dominated armament planning to such a great extent that even serious deficiencies particularly the problem of officer personnel were accepted, not to mention their effects in the field of finance and on the armament industry.[46] If one considers Fritsch's statement in his letter to Blomberg of 12 October 1936 according to which Hitler demanded 'a powerful army in the shortest possible time', i.e. without fixing a definite date, one may assume that the military commanders and especially the Reich Defence Minister were responsible for the choice of date.

The underlying significance of the August programme was not confined to the military sphere alone. Although the military planners doubtless paid less and less attention to the political and economic aspects of their actions these, nevertheless, did not lose their significance. Research into National Socialist economic policies has revealed in detail that from the very beginning rearmament determined to an increasing extent the objectives and methods of economic activities.[47] This development reached its first high point in 1936. With the announcement of the Four-Year Plan at the Party rally on 9 September Hitler publicly declared his intention to gear the economy entirely to rearmament.[48] The relationship between the military and the economic programme of summer 1936 has not yet been investigated in detail. The fact that they run so parallel is striking and leads one to believe that both were the result of a decision taken in the spring.

On the basis of a directive issued by Hitler, Göring was commissioned at the beginning of April to review and improve the situation regarding raw materials and foreign exchange. One month later the Raw Materials and Foreign Exchange Staff, which may be considered as a forerunner of the Four-Year Plan, began its work.[49] Blomberg and the Armed Forces Office participated to a considerable degree in the deliberations and decisions taken in this

TABLE 3.3.   Armaments Planning and the Level of Army Armament[52]

	Strength of army under Treaty of Versailles	December programme 1933	August programme 1936	Strength of army at outbreak of war
Infantry divs.	7	21	32	35
Infantry divs. (motorised)	—	—	4	4
Mountain brig./div.	—	—	1	/3
Cavalry brig./div.	/3	1/3	1/	1/
Armoured unit/div.	—	1/	/3	/6
Light div.	—	1	3	4
Strength of the peacetime army	100,000	300,000	830,000	730,000
Strength of the wartime army	—	63 Div.	4,620,000	3,737,000
Strength of the field army	—	33 Div.	102 Div.-Units	103 Div.-Units

field. Fully aware of the tight economic situation, Blomberg ordered the Commander-in-Chief of the Army to compile a comprehensive plan at the end of May/early June which was available in draft form in August and was also shown to Blomberg. At the end of August Blomberg wrote to Göring suggesting that future financial requirements for rearmament purposes be discussed by the Raw Materials and Foreign Exchange Staff. In this context he mentioned figures which roughly corresponded to the requirements of the plan for the build-up of the Army.[50] Due to the fact that Blomberg undertook extensive studies on the economic aspects of rearmament we may assume that he also spoke to Hitler on this matter. This assumption is supported by Schacht's dramatic appeal that Blomberg might try to dissuade Hitler at the last moment from proclaiming his economic programme at the Party congress. Blomberg not only failed to fulfil this request but hoped that due to the measures announced in Hitler's memorandum with which he was familiar all the Army's difficulties could be overcome.[51]

Even if on the basis of this evidence it can be demonstrated that Blomberg dealt equally with both components of rearmament, i.e. the military and economic, evidence that planning was co-ordinated is still lacking. It is a fact however that German armaments policy after the full restoration of military sovereignty in spring 1936 was based on new principles with the adoption of the August programme of the Army High Command and Hitler's Four-Year Plan. Hitler's stipulation at the end of his memorandum on the Four-Year Plan that 'within four years . . . the German Army . . . must be operational' and 'the German economy . . . prepared for war' was not mere rhetoric but rather a definite instruction on how to proceed that had already been taken into account by the Army's planners. Half a year after the reoccupation of the Rhineland the Army's August programme had set the course for the second phase of Hitler's policy towards the realisation of his expansionist aims.

4 The Growth of the *Luftwaffe*

Between 1933 and 1939 Germany's neighbouring states regarded the build-up of the *Luftwaffe* as the most dangerous existing threat to their security. The aeroplane even more than the tank was viewed as the offensive weapon of the future, its potential effects seeming to embody both the totality and the brutality of modern warfare. Viewed from the outside the air force of the Third Reich was the work of Hermann Göring, the most powerful man after Adolf Hitler in the hierarchy of Party and State. It is reasonable to suppose therefore that the build-up of this section of the armed forces and in particular its armament and operational planning were carried out in accordance with the régime's short- and long-term political aims.

The ideas evolved within the framework of the armed forces' general armament planning for the future development of an air force were in the main centred upon the employment of airborne forces as a support arm for both the Army and the Navy.[1] The appointment of Göring as *Reichskommissar* for Aviation and of Erhard Milch as Secretary of State at the *Reichskommissariat*, however marked a fundamental turning point in this concept. The setting up of the Ministry of Aviation in May 1933 had decided once and for all the question of the *Luftwaffe* as an independent and separate service within the armed forces.[2] It was Göring's political weight within the National Socialist movement, the various functions he performed and his influence within the government machinery that made this speedy decision possible. It goes almost without saying that the *Luftwaffe*'s changed status opened up new perspectives both in armament objectives and in armament planning.

In May 1933 Milch received a memorandum from Dr Robert Knauss, director of Lufthansa, entitled 'The German Air Fleet'. It contained certain ideas with which Milch declared himself to be in complete agreement.[3] Milch's approval of this memorandum can be taken as the earliest competent statement to come to light on the basic principles of air force armament and the direction of air warfare which corresponded to views held within the leadership of the Reich Aviation Ministry.

Knauss proceeded from the political assumption that the goal of the 'national government' was to re-establish 'Germany's position as a major power in Europe' and that this goal could be achieved only by arming her to a level that would 'at least afford the chance of success in a war on two fronts against France and Poland'. Knauss felt that the 'critical period of time' before this armament objective could be realised could be shortened 'by no other more effective means than by the creation of a strong air force'. He considered that 'the essential significance of the *Luftwaffe* as a weapon of war' lay 'in the far reaching and operationally flexible striking power of bomber aircraft united in the air fleet'. An air force of this character would 'at a stroke . . . considerably increase . . . the risks of war' for any potential enemy and reduce the danger of a preventive strike against a Germany of renewed military strength. The striking feature of this concept of a 'risk air force'[4] was not only the fact that it was a revival of the military theory developed by Admiral von Tirpitz but that it bore a close resemblance to Hitler's statement to the *Reichswehr* generals on 3 February 1933 which dealt in particular with the power-political objectives of the régime and which gave an appraisal of the state of foreign policy and its risks. Knauss as Director of Lufthansa was articulating something which was clearly a common conviction among the military leadership although the highest-ranking army and naval officers never mentioned it outright.[5] Unlike the Army and the Navy leaders, he was able to offer a solution to the problem of how armament could be effected despite the risk of serious international developments.

In concrete terms Knauss recommended the early and clandestine formation of an air force of approximately 390 four-engined bombers, to be supplemented by 10 air reconnaissance squadrons. He felt that with the co-operation of army aviation units and the Lufthansa Organisation it would be possible to make 'the necessary arrangements in terms of personnel and equipment to effect the surprise consolidation of an air force within a short time'. Knauss was convinced that an extremely flexible military instrument of the kind envisaged would guarantee Germany vital advantages in any conflict with France and Poland but even more important he expected the risk air force to have a deterrent effect.

For the sake of military objectives Knauss pleaded vigorously in favour of an armament policy based on certain clearly defined priorities. An 'even distribution of the armament effort over all areas' would result in a 'dissipation of resources' and thereby increase the threat of a preventive strike. During the 'risk phase' of German rearmament the accelerated formation of five army divisions or the construction of two pocket battleships would bring about only a minor change in the European balance of forces. Knauss' statement was clearly aimed against the Navy's known ship-building plans.[6] In an explicit rejection of the naval policy developed by Tirpitz and in the interest of national defence, Knauss maintained that the Navy should have nothing beyond a defensive function in the Baltic and the North Sea. He stated that the resources needed to build two pocket battleships would suffice to 'build up an air force of 400 large bombers' which would assure Germany 'air superiority in central Europe within the next few years'. Knauss' memorandum also spelled out some clearly defined priorities within the field of air armament itself. Remarkably enough he flatly denied fighter aircraft a strategic function, describing them merely as a support arm of the Army and Navy. His all-important objective was the build-up of a bomber fleet and supporting reconnaissance squadrons.

Knauss rounded off his appeal in favour of a risk air force and of its paramount importance for the success of the general armament programme by adding some political considerations. He pointed out that the notion of independent operative air warfare was gaining more support both in Italy and France. Any hesitation would therefore 'reduce the lead of anything up to 10 years which Germany might gain by the creation of an air force at this point' and that everything depended on 'precisely this decade'. And Knauss was confident that 'the tremendous energy of the national government' and 'the qualities of leadership of the first German Minister of Aviation' provided the best guarantee that the 'life or death decision' involved in air armament would be taken promptly and that all resistance to its implementation would be overcome.

Although Milch showed he was in agreement with its content, the impact of this memorandum upon the *Luftwaffe*'s armament plans cannot be precisely defined. In June 1933 Milch submitted a provisional programme which was approved by Göring and Blomberg before the month was out.[7] This programme, which underwent only minor alterations in August and September, reflected only in part the ideas developed by Knauss: it did not accept his recommendation that the planned 'Air Fleet' of some 600 front-line aircraft should consist of a single type of heavily armed bomber, nor did it propose the size of air fleet he had envisaged.

On the other hand it is clear that in its basic features the programme was based on the notion of a risk air force. The bomber squadrons formed the nucleus of the future air force and were intended to fulfil the roles of political intimidation and military deterrence envisaged by Knauss.

Without going more deeply at this juncture into the military ramifications of the programme, it is nevertheless possible to conclude with some certainty from the political reaction to the build-up of the *Luftwaffe* that it did fulfil its given *political* task in a manner which far exceeded the objectives Knauss set. His air force was conceived as a weapon against the Reich's European neighbours in particular France and Poland. Yet paradoxically the emergent *Luftwaffe* had the greatest political effect on that European power which Knauss had never even mentioned in his memorandum and which could not even be effectively threatened by the air warfare resources proposed by the first German armament programme: Great Britain. As early as the summer of 1933 the first signs of concern in British public opinion became evident.[8] These increased as a result of internal political events in Germany and the withdrawal of the Reich from the League of Nations and the disarmament conference. The air threat to the British Isles and the dramatic description of all its possible aspects soon became a permanent topic in the media. Stanley Baldwin's declaration before the House of Commons on 30 July 1934 that in view of the progress made in military aviation the defence of Britain would no longer begin at the White Cliffs of Dover but instead on the Rhine marked the first peak in this general obsession.[9]

The modest air arm had created a political situation which allowed Hitler to negotiate from a position of relative strength on the question of an air pact with Great Britain.[10] During the first phase of its build-up which was based on the principles developed by Knauss, the risk air force had in fact produced its intended political effects. These, however, went beyond the scope originally intended and exceeded the initially limited military objectives.

Knauss had written his memorandum at a time when the initial organisational decisions, based on military criteria, on the build-up of a separate service had already been made. The personnel and material requirements, however, still needed clarification. In as much as the terms of the Treaty of Versailles were still in effect, expansion only seemed possible if all executive departments of the State, especially the *Reichswehr* and the Reich Ministry of Transport, extended their active support to the new service.

This was particularly true in the case of personnel recruitment. Defence Minister von Blomberg proved to be the driving force here, an indication that he was fully aware of the significance of this new section of the armed forces and of its military and political functions. Blomberg took advantage of the Commanders' conference convened after the establishment of the Air Ministry to point out that 'the air officer corps' should become an 'elite corps of bold spirit' whose 'preferential treatment in all areas' was necessary, a fact which the other branches of the *Wehrmacht* should recognise.[11] At the beginning of October 1933 after the ground had been thus prepared and planning in the Air Ministry had taken on a more concrete form, the Defence Minister notified the generals on what scale the Army and Navy were to contribute to the recruitment of *Luftwaffe* personnel. Blomberg emphasised[12] that nothing could be 'more short-sighted . . . than the selection of poor personnel'. On the contrary the *Luftwaffe* called for the 'crème de la crème'. Subsequently at several top-level military meetings Blomberg spoke emphatically on behalf of the *Luftwaffe*'s personnel requirements and did not rule out the possibility of using coercion.

The extent of the problems requiring solution may best be illustrated by referring to the growth rate of the Air Force's officer corps and that of total personnel strength. At the time its existence was revealed early in 1935 the corps consisted of 900 flying officers and 200 anti-aircraft artillery officers in command of approximately 17,000 non-commissioned officers and men. Two and a half years later at the end of 1937 the officer corps had increased in size to over five times the 1935 figure. Counting all three arms of the service there was a total of slightly over 6000 officers. By August 1939 the corps finally grew to a strength of over 15,000 officers in charge of about 370,000 non-commissioned officers and men.[13] Thus since its existence had been revealed, that is, in as little as four and a half years, the officer corps of the *Luftwaffe* increased to over thirteen times its original strength. Considering that this officer corps did not have the relatively broad homogenous basis of the Army's, the existence of that cohesion necessary for the effective performance of military funtion must be viewed with scepticism. One condition which may be regarded as having aggravated the situation was the fact that all high-ranking *Luftwaffe* officers had of necessity been army officers formerly. These officers were, at least initially, somewhat sceptical as to the extent of the operational capacities of independent air warfare. But most important of all, they were totally inexperienced in the command and control of major airborne units.[14] In this connection a problem can be identified which resulted from the build-up phase and could not be overcome by the time the war broke out. It should be noted that Dr Knauss the Traffic Manager of *Lufthansa* makes no mention at all in his memorandum of the personnel problems inherent in the practicalities of commanding the risk air force.

An even greater burden than these unavoidable weaknesses regarding the quality of personnel came in the shape of great difficulties regarding material resources. Armament planning and production had to expect to contend with considerable uncertainties.

According to a directive of 12 July 1933 on the first phase of formation, a total of 26 squadrons was to be set up as independent airborne units, although, 'maintaining maximum possible secrecy' the units being located alongside civil aviation facilities.[15] The emphasis of the programme was placed on the 10 projected bomber squadrons plus an additional 7 reconnaissance and 7 fighter squadrons. A month and a half later on 28 August 1933 Milch signed the programme for the second 1935 formation phase. It provided for a further 29 combat units to be brought into service by 1 October 1935. Of these 17 were intended as bomber squadrons while only 8 and 4 were to be reconnaissance and fighter squadrons respectively.[16] A glance at the number of aircraft delivered by the end of 1934 shows that industry had managed to meet its delivery schedules as planned. By the end of that year air units had been equipped with 270 bombers, 99 fighter aircraft and 303 reconnaissance aircraft. A much greater number – approximately 1300 aircraft – were used for training and other purposes.[17]

This was a great achievement on the part of an aircraft industry which had been expecially hard hit by the Depression. At the end of January 1933 the manufacturers of aircraft fuselages and engines who formed the National Association of the German Aircraft Industry employed a staff of slightly less than 4000.[18] Although the major companies – Junkers in Dessau, Heinkel in Warnemünde, Dornier in Friedrichshafen and the Bavarian Aircraft Corporation in Augsburg – had done much in the field of the design and development of new aircraft, their production capacity was nevertheless extremely limited. With the appointment of Milch as Secretary of State, however, a man had emerged to direct the Ministry who, himself a former director of *Lufthansa*, was familiar with the industry and well able to assess the situation in respect of the projected armament programme. In addition to the considerable financial means necessary for the expansion of production, the build-up of an air force comparable to those of the other European powers depended more than anything else upon rationalisation.

In early June 1933 decisive ministerial discussions took place at which Schacht, President of the Reichsbank, explained to Hitler his plan to finance the job-creation programme and rearmament by means of the renowned Mefo bills.[19] This plan also provided the vehicle for funding the expansion of the aircraft industry's production capacity. The various initiatives of the Ministry were reflected in the ever-increasing number of employees in the industry. From 4000 in January 1933 the figures climbed to 16,870 in early 1934 and reached 59,600 on 1 April 1935. One year later the number had risen to 110,600; on 1 April 1937 it was approximately 167,200 and finally on 1 October 1938 the figure stood at 204,100 employees. This number does not include the equipment supply and repair industries.[20] Within only five and a half years the industry's manpower potential had increased by 50 times.

The rationalisation of production also resulted from an initiative by the Ministry of Aviation. Best known in this area is the development that took place at Junkers. The firm worked out the well-known ABC programme which was implemented about the end of 1933 when the Ju 52 went into production. It provided for the production of components by a number of contractors working under the direction and overall supervision of the Junkers Corporation. The only work done in the firm's main plant in Dessau was the final assembly of the aircraft. This method constituted an important step towards the objective of the functional organisation of the parts supply industry. At the same time it initiated cooperation between aircraft manufacturers who had hitherto been very anxious to maintain their own independence. Moreover it also paved the way for the licensed production of aircraft which was to become more and more important in the following years. For instance during the period 1933–1945 a total of 17,552 Junkers aircraft were built under licence by other companies.[21]

In this way Milch and the Technical Office at the Reich Ministry of Aviation under Colonel Wimmer had in close co-operation with the manufacturers established the industrial production base for the construction of an air force in an amazingly short time. The question remained, however, as to which dimensions and technical specifications the build-up was to be effected. As early as August 1933 Milch had announced a further 'Comprehensive Armament Programme 1934–8' which was to give 'due consideration both to the *requirements of national defence and technical possibilitie*s'.[22] The organisational, personnel and industrial requirements for its implementation had been created by the beginning of 1934. The military function of the *Luftwaffe* had become more evident as a result of the 1933/4 *Wehrmacht* studies which had revealed the need to strengthen air defence forces.[23] The aircraft acquisition programme of 1 July 1934 was accordingly based on these requirements. This was the first long-term programme and called for the acquisition of 17,015 aircraft of all types for the period up to 31 March 1938.[24] The significance attached to the programme is underlined by the fact that Hitler had Göring, Milch and the administrative heads within the Ministry of Aviation brief him on its content. In late August 1934 Hitler approved the cost estimates for the programme which were in the region of 10·5 thousand million Reichsmarks.[25]

It should be noted that the huge number of aircraft to be acquired under the terms of the programme included only 6671 combat aircraft which were divided into the following categories:[26]

    2225 fighter aircraft
    2188 bombers
     699 dive bombers
    1559 reconnaissance aircraft

The ratio of combat aircraft to training aircraft – the programme provided for 8941 trainers – reflects the awareness of the *Luftwaffe* leadership that the years to come were to be devoted primarily to the consolidation of the service and that training in all fields would be of the utmost importance. The surprising degree of preference given to the fighter section was a consequence of the 1933/4 *Wehrmacht* winter studies which had stressed the importance of the air defence component within the overall programme. The programme was in line with the concept of an operational air force as developed by Blomberg in his directive of August 1933.[27]

According to this it was to be the task of the so-called 'operational *Luftwaffe*', in the case of a European war on several fronts against France, Belgium, Poland and Czechoslovakia, to take over an operational function within the framework of overall strategy. This task was to be carried out either independently and with the support of long-range reconnaissance squadrons or in conjunction with the Army and Navy.

During the programme's first operative phase up to 30 September 1935 a total of 4021 aircraft were to be delivered to the *Luftwaffe*. In order to achieve this objective the monthly production rate was to be increased from 72 aircraft in January 1934 to 293 aircraft by July 1935. In other words, the industry was expected to increase its output four-fold within a relatively short time. By the end of December 1934, 1959 aircraft had already been delivered to the service, the backlog on the delivery schedule amounting to only 6 per cent! It seemed that the industrial planners of the Reich Ministry of Aviation had in fact achieved an outstanding performance because it appeared that both the planning schedule and industrial production capacity matched almost perfectly.[28]

In his directive of 28 August 1933 Milch had laid down two principles on which the overall programme for the 1934–8 period was to be based. It was to satisfy the requirements of national defence and also to give due consideration to technical possibilities.[29] The astonishing ability to keep up to schedule together with the unquestionable deterrent effect abroad – whatever means had been used to achieve it – provided proof that the *Luftwaffe* had satisfactorily met the demands of national defence during those years. To what extent, however, did the overall programme in fact take account of technical possibilities? The 270 bombers delivered by the end of 1934 were Ju 52 and Do 11 aircraft and the 99 single-seater fighter planes were Ar 64 and Ar 65 biplanes. Both the units using these aircraft and the Reich Ministry of Aviation agreed that these machines were no longer up to existing standards of technology. Milch also was fully aware of this situation. He had rejected Hitler's demand for a further increase in production figures with the argument that this would lead to too many obsolescent models being produced. New aircraft were already in the development stage especially the medium-range bombers Do 17, He 111 and Ju 86 as well as the Ju 87 dive bomber. The question was, however, when the time-consuming development and test phase would eventually come to an end so that these aircraft could go into production. In addition, aircraft engine development and production had reached a serious bottleneck. It was in this field that the resources of the Ministry, which had been so successful in creating the production base for the fuselages, reached the limits of their effectiveness. Efforts to increase the production base in this area were also promoted to the greatest extent possible. But the requirement voiced by Major von Richthofen at a meeting with the manufacturers on 20 and 21 September 1934, that the research and development period of a new engine would have to be reduced from five or six years to only two, simply failed to acknowledge the hard facts of life.[30]

It is quite obvious that the conversion to new and better aircraft which Milch and the Technical Office had been pursuing since at least 1934 did not materialise as planned. The development and testing of new models and the development of engines and their production turned out to be processes which could be controlled and preplanned only to a limited extent. The Ministry planners had up to that point pushed the production of aircraft which would soon become obsolete, not only in the interests of national defence but also because this was the only approach which would create an efficient industry. In as much as the first tangible success on the way toward this objective had materialised in late 1934 and early 1935, conversion had to be a phased process if they wished to avoid the risk of bringing production to a standstill until the new model was ready to go into production. It is against this background that we should consider the various supplementary programmes of 1935 and the first half of 1936. Despite all difficulties, planning retained a remarkable degree of flexibility until well into the summer of 1936.[31] For instance, production of the Ju 52, which had been considered an expedient solution from the very beginning, was continued until the new bomber models were ready to go into production. Thereafter the Ju 52 became the *Luftwaffe*'s most important transport aircraft.

On the other hand, however, flexibility was combined with a marked degree of uncertainty as to what technological and military requirements should be established for the various categories of aircraft. This in turn had a lasting effect on the development process.

The problem had come to light in connection with the new models of the twin-engined bomber[32] and was also to affect the four-engined strategic bomber project which had been on the minds of the Army leadership concerned with military aviation since the days of the *Reichswehr*. Colonel Wever, the Head of the Air Staff Command who had intensively studied the problems of air warfare, soon recognised the importance of this project and as early as May 1934 Junkers and Dornier were awarded a development contract. The four-engined strategic bomber was supposed to go into production in 1938. However, even before the Ju 89 and Do 19 had completed their test flights, doubts arose as to whether the speed and range of these aircraft would be sufficient to satisfy military requirements. Here again the problem of engine design was of critical importance. On 17 April 1936 Wever signed guidelines for the future development of the strategic bomber which the present prototypes had been unable to satisfy. The result was that the development of the four-engined bomber was delayed and Wever's death on 3 June 1936 was another set-back. Eventually it was deleted completely from the general development programme.[33]

Wever's death marked the end of an important phase in the build-up of the *Luftwaffe*. The period from 1933 to 1936 had been characterised by the activities of a number of capable officers occupying the key positions in the Reich Ministry of Aviation, which in turn had been more under Milch's direction than Göring's. In addition to the successful development of the aircraft industry which was largely the work of Milch, Wimmer and Kesselring, Wever more than anybody else deserves credit for reconsidering and redefining the designated military task of the *Luftwaffe* under new conditions which offered it wider scope. A General Staff officer of the Army and former chief of the training department of the Army Command, Wever – like Milch – had familiarised himself within a surprisingly short time with the strategic and tactical aspects of air warfare structured round a bomber fleet as described by Knauss in his memorandum. As a result all the armament programmes for which he shared responsibility were marked by one feature namely that the bomber was given priority.

Wever's views were clearly set out in the *Luftwaffe*'s service directive, 'Aerial Warfare' (L. Dv. 16) published in 1936. In it the *Luftwaffe* had progressed from being merely a risk air force which had ensured that Germany could safely rearm.[34] The directive reflected the belief that the single most important task of the *Luftwaffe* lay in an offensive against the broadly defined 'combat strength of the enemy' and of 'its population's will to resist'. Out of

this general description of the *Luftwaffe*'s function there emerged
three main tasks stated in the directive in the following order:
(1) 'to combat the enemy air force'; (2) to give direct support to
Army and Navy operations; (3) 'to strike at the sources of power of
the enemy's armed forces' and to cut off the 'flow of power' to the
front. The *Luftwaffe*'s combat operations were to hit the 'enemy's
population and country' at their most sensitive points or 'at the
roots' as it was expressed elsewhere in the directive. Thus in its own
view the *Luftwaffe* had gone far beyond the role of a mere support
force for the Army and Navy. This was clearly shown by the action
of the Condor Legion in Spain.[35] The 1936 directive brought
together all the ingredients of modern air warfare. The diverse
nature of its possible uses however led to the conclusion that aerial
warfare could only be considered within the overall framework of
general warfare: 'Those in charge of overall strategy should retain a
firm influence over air force objectives'. Closer inspection shows
that the collaboration between the *Luftwaffe* and the Army and
Navy was marked by some degree of uncertainty. Nevertheless a
comparison of Wever's thoughts on air warfare with corresponding
contemporary statements made within the leading circles of the two
other services shows unmistakeably that the airman, in contrast to
his colleagues, still retained a broader overall view that the
Luftwaffe's course should be one which combined both independent
and co-operative action.

Immediately after Wever's death, Göring took two decisions on
staff changes which marked the beginning of the disintegration of
the hitherto unified and effective structure of the *Luftwaffe* leadership. Lieutenant General Albert Kesselring, previously Head of
Luftwaffe Administration, succeeded Wever as Head of the *Luftwaffe*
Staff Command and General Wimmer was replaced as Head of the
Technical Office by Udet, a fighter pilot and stunt flyer. Kesselring
enjoyed a high reputation as an expert organiser and effective
administrator but as the Chief of the General Staff it seems he did
not prove the best choice. Udet had been talked into joining the
Luftwaffe after 1933, had last held the rank of Colonel, and was
Chief of Staff of the fighter and dive-bomber squadrons. Apart
from his wealth of experience as an aviator, however, he lacked the
technical and managerial capabilities which the new office
demanded. These top-level changes were accompanied by a rapid
series of organisational changes. The establishment of new areas of
competence was combined with overt and covert curtailment of

former responsibilities and an inflation of the entire apparatus.[36] To
a certain extent it may have been simply a case of natural growth
but the increased influence of Göring as the Commander-in-Chief
of the *Luftwaffe* should be seen as a new factor.

These top level changes came at a time when the conversion of
the *Luftwaffe* to new aircraft with all its inherent problems was in full
swing and when production began to feel the increasing pressure of
the general lack of raw materials. Moreover they came at a time
when Great Britain, whose reaction to the build-up of German air
power had been clear from the start, was beginning to be included
in the tactical planning activities of the *Luftwaffe*.

The necessity apparent since 1934 of equipping the *Luftwaffe* as
quickly as possible with the more up-to-date flying equipment
could only be fully met in 1937. At this point the Ministry of
Aviation was already thinking in terms of a second conversion phase
in which, for example, the bomber types He 111 and Do 17, and
even the fighter Me 109, introduced by this stage were to be
replaced by more advanced aircraft. This renewed period of
conversion was scheduled to begin in 1939 and to be more or less
completed in 1940.[37] In view of the increased complexity of the
equipment and its technical sophistication, the selection of new
aircraft models became a very intricate process and production was
likely to become an enterprise extremely prone to interruption.
Udet demanded simple, straightforward, sturdy and readily main-
tainable aircraft but failed to point out at the same time that fully
developed and engineered products are normally the result of a long
and intensive research and development phase and even more
important, of rigid testing.[38] Of all the resources provided for
industry by the Ministry of Aviation, time was the one in shortest
supply. The second armament conversion phase, with its unavoidable limitation of the types of aircraft, turned out to be an extremely
risky undertaking under these conditions.

In the course of 1938 the realisation gained ground in the
Luftwaffe leadership that Great Britain should be considered a
potential adversary and that consequently it would be necessary to
find or develop an aircraft that would fulfil the requirements of air
warfare against Britain as an island. Both of the standard aircraft
already in use, the He 111 and the Do 17, failed to qualify for the
task both in terms of their range and bomb-carrying capacity. This
marked the beginning of the twin-engined Ju 88. In accordance
with the specification of the *Luftwaffe* Staff Command and of the

Technical Office, the aircraft had been developed in 1936 as a high-speed bomber. In the summer of 1937 it was tested and in the spring of 1938 entered the production planning phase.[39] When the Ju 88 was considered and eventually selected as the successor to the He 111 and Do 17, the requirements which the military imposed upon the design began to grow. The most aggravating requirement laid down by the General Staff and endorsed by Udet was that the high-speed bomber should not only be capable of carrying two tons of bombs over a distance of 2000 miles but that, in addition, it should be able to deliver its load by dive-bombing. There is no doubt that this type of bombing would have been much more effective and economical than area bombing, given the bomb sights available. Since the early thirties Udet himself had been an advocate of dive-bombing,[40] and the Condor Legion operating in Spain had demonstrated its effectiveness. Since then however the idea had become an obsession. The military requirements proved to have a disastrous impact on the flight characteristics of the Ju 88: its weight increased from 7 to 12 tons and its speed dropped from almost 312 m.p.h. to a little less than 187 m.p.h. It has even been alleged that an astonishing total of 250,000 engineering design changes were made to the original prototype. The first example of the new model underwent its maiden flight on 18 June 1938. A month before this the Technical Office had already included production as of November 1938 in their programme![41] This whole process, like the subsequent development of the Ju 88 programme, can only be described as the corruption of technical and industrial development and planning by new military objectives.

It goes without saying that these deficiencies, and in some instances the inability to master the advanced technology involved, were bound to have repercussions upon both production and productivity. It comes as no surprise therefore that actual aircraft production figures for 1938 indicate a sharp decrease.[42] This was partly attributable to the general shortage of raw materials which the *Luftwaffe* first began to feel in 1936. The fact that after the Munich conference the planned monthly production rate in Germany decreased while it increased in other European countries indicates that the arms programme had reached the limits of economic capacity. This fact could not be altered by the highly ambitious objectives of the numerous programmes.

The question remains as to what military objectives lay behind the *Luftwaffe*'s armament programme and whether the service which had proved such a political success also possessed the military capacity to fulfil the expectations placed in it. Knauss had developed his idea of a bomber fleet on the assumption of a European war on two fronts against Poland and France and this constellation was also used in the '*Wehrmacht* Study of 1935/6' in which Czechoslovakia took the place of Poland.[43] According to the study the *Luftwaffe* would be able to accomplish its mission against Czechoslovakia although the *Luftwaffe* Staff Command under Wever also concluded that 'it would be defeated in the long run by the numerically far stronger French air force'. Intensified training at all levels of command and improvement of infrastructure especially of the alternative air fields to be used in emergencies (the so-called 'E-bases') were deemed necessary.[44] A consolidation phase however took top priority. But the conversion programme which had required the full time and attention of the *Luftwaffe* in 1937 constituted a major handicap for any such consolidation. Only after completion of the conversion programme and after qualitative improvement of materials, infrastructure and training achieved up to that point did the *Luftwaffe* appear to have a chance of successfully accomplishing its mission in a European war fought on several fronts.

But the turn against Great Britain in 1937 resulted in a significant expansion of military objectives. As far as operations were concerned, the earliest evidence of this change is the 'Advance Orientation' of 18 February 1938 of the Chief of the Staff Command concerning the objectives of air warfare in the west.[45] This paper identified British air bases in eastern England, the port of London and its munitions industry and the English Channel ports as the target of a future tactical mission. On 4 May 1938 Lieutenant Colonel Jeschonnek, the Chief of the *Luftwaffe* Staff Command, and Commander Heye of the operational section of the Naval Command held a meeting[46] which revealed that the Air Force Staff entertained the idea of occupying the Netherlands and Belgium as a base from which to conduct air operations against England and a 'strategic raid' on the British Navy. Jeschonnek also hoped that a campaign against the United Kingdom would be facilitated should Italy decide to enter the war. Altogether, these ideas were still rather general, but they assumed a more substantial shape in the memorandum of 22 September 1938 from General Felmy, Commander of Air Group Command 2, and in the exercises of the 2nd Air Fleet in May 1939 which he directed.[47] Felmy's realistic views on the still unresolved command and control problems of air warfare overseas and the training of crews, which was insufficient to enable them to cope with the special conditions inherent in operations over the British Isles, not to mention the insufficient range of penetration of the available bombers, could lead to only one conclusion: the *Luftwaffe* was not yet ready to accomplish the new mission assigned to it. Even the proposed mass production of the Ju 88 could not have altered this conclusion for a long time to come.

In the face of the stagnation of aircraft production experienced in 1937 and 1938, it would have been only logical first to eliminate the various causes of the crisis, except of course for the general shortage of raw materials, which was beyond control. However, the opposite happened. At the end of 1936 Göring demanded that industry should produce at mobilisation levels, and in autumn 1938 Hitler ordered the *Luftwaffe* to be enlarged to five times its size.[48] In the case of a highly complex project such as the *Luftwaffe*'s armament programme, the recipe for overcoming crises by making excessive demands was bound to fail or to say the least have a negative effect. The politically motivated armament demands had not in any way altered the fact that the fuel stockpile available to the *Luftwaffe* at the outbreak of war would last only for a little less than two months. In addition the *Luftwaffe* now faced a new adversary in Great Britain.

By the time war broke out political developments had caught up with the *Luftwaffe*; developments which it had itself largely promoted in the initial years of the Third Reich. In an astonishingly short space of time it had succeeded in meeting the requirements necessary to fulfil the primary military task of tactical warfare in the event of a European war on several fronts. However the international consequences of rearmament, and in particular the build-up of the *Luftwaffe* itself, had led to a redefinition of the military objectives. These were now beyond the *Luftwaffe*'s means to fulfil both as far as command and control and as far as armament technology were concerned. The risk air force itself had contributed its share in precipitating a political risk which it could no longer master militarily.

5 The Armament Aims of the German Navy

From 1933 onwards the rearmament of the Army and *Luftwaffe* was characterised by a steady expansion of the scope and aims of their individual programmes and by their acceleration and demands for rapid results. This meant that between 1933–9 Admiral Raeder and the Navy leadership faced almost insoluble problems. Tirpitz himself had never tired of stressing that a fleet could not be built in a day but rather required decades, an opinion shared by Raeder.[1] The question whether the Navy could strike a balance between, on the one hand, the necessarily long-term nature of naval armament and, on the other, the tempo set by Hitler and the other two services in their attempt to restore Germany's Great Power status depended not least on the armaments goals fixed for the Navy by its own leadership.

The Treaty of Versailles had limited the size of the German Fleet to 6 battleships of the pre-Dreadnought era, 6 cruisers, 12 destroyers and 12 torpedo boats. In addition 2 battleships, 2 cruisers, 4 destroyers and 4 torpedo boats which were neither to be armed nor manned were designated reserve units. The treaty had also laid down the schedule for and the upper limit of any replacement shipbuilding that might become necessary to maintain this fleet.[2] At the beginning of 1933 the Navy's level of armament differed fundamentally from the Army's in that the 1100 officers, 13,900 non-commissioned officers and men did not even possess the naval hardware permitted by the Treaty of Versailles. The light naval forces were the only section which had almost reached the limit set by the treaty. Between 1925 and 1931, five modern light cruisers had been brought into service and these were available alongside 12 torpedo boats, although the latter had been built on as large a scale as permitted by the Allies' regulations governing destroyers. The process of replacing the battleships of the Tirpitz era with new ones of the 'Deutschland' class – the pocket battleships of 10,000 tons –

had, only just begun however. Orders had been placed for three of these although none had as yet been completed.[3] This unsatisfactory level of armament reveals the exceptional position in which the Navy in many respects found itself. Public opinion if it took any notice of the Navy at all only occasionally defined its role as going beyond defending the coast, preserving the Reich's link with East Prussia and keeping the Baltic open.

This in no way corresponded to the views of the Navy chiefs under Raeder who held to the Tirpitzian tradition of grand strategy. Despite the inadequate level of naval armament, they had for years concerned themselves with the operational problems of a war on several fronts regarding their primary task as one of an 'offensively' conducted defence of Germany's shipping routes. This meant that the Atlantic was considered as a potential zone of operations.[4] The unavoidable gap – which characterised all planning efforts – between existing circumstances and future possibilities had already assumed dangerous proportions in the Navy by this stage.

A different emphasis was to be found in the naval conversion plan approved by the Reich Defence Minister on 15 November 1932. Running parallel to the phases of the Army's conversion plan,[5] the scope for rearmament within the limitations of the Treaty of Versailles was to be fully exploited by early 1938. In addition one aircraft carrier and a first series of submarines were to be brought into service followed by the creation of a fleet air arm. These fairly modest plans encountered some criticism within the Navy itself since it was felt that 'the opportunity of satisfying urgent requirements after years of having our hands tied' had not been 'fully exploited'.[6] Yet the conversion plan had nevertheless provided for an increase in the number of officers and men without which no grand conception was possible. The special emphasis the plan laid on the development of the submarine and the fleet air arm tended to counteract the undue influence of the Tirpitz era's legacy of naval strategy.

In Hitler, a politician had been appointed Reich Chancellor at the end of January 1933 who, in his political writings and in numerous speeches, made no secret of the fact that he was an out-and-out critic of Tirpitz's naval policy, that he believed a naval emphasis in German policy to be of no value whatsoever, and that he would be satisfied if no more than a 'navy for coastal protection' existed for the sake of avoiding conflict with Britain. For Raeder and the Navy's high-ranking officers this was an intolerable state of affairs.[7] Thus it was of decisive importance for the future of the Navy how the relationship between its leaders and the new military and political leadership would develop. At least Neurath and Blomberg viewed the Navy sympathetically. Göring, on the other hand, in his influential position in the Party and State and in his new capacity as *Reichskommissar* for Aviation very quickly became a new and powerful rival for the Navy.[8]

The earliest known fairly detailed discussion between Hitler and Raeder must be assessed against this background. The meeting probably took place early in April 1933. Raeder may well have intended to go beyond the subject of immediate interest, namely how to tackle the problems which might result from the British Prime Minister MacDonald's disarmament proposals, in order to familiarise the Chancellor with the military and political aspects of the Navy's current expansion and to win him over to its aims.[9] The precise course of the conversation which dealt in detail with diplomatic affairs cannot be fully reconstructed from the record. The Head of the Naval Command clearly defined the provisional target of fleet construction. It appeared to be extremely modest since Raeder declared himself in agreement with the number of ships specified by Versailles even though elsewhere he mentioned the need to build submarines and an aircraft carrier exactly in accordance with the conversion plan. What mattered to him was to be free to decide the tonnage of the ships in accordance with the agreement on 'equality of status' reached in Geneva in 1932. This led to the specific demand that the construction of the new battleship 'D', planned for 1934, should be based on a tonnage and armament which would guarantee that it would be a match for its new French counterpart, the 'Dunkerque'.

The political arguments which begin and conclude the record of the conversation are also of great interest since they sum up the larger issues in a few words. Raeder was aware that Hitler rejected a forced naval rearmament, above all, because of the political consequences this would have for his policy towards Britain. Raeder therefore declared right at the outset that the Navy never had any intention of regarding Britain as an enemy[10] and at the end of his notes he wrote down, '*Bündnisfähigkeit*' (prospects for alliances) and underlined it. In doing this he showed himself to be a disciple of his former commanding officer, the masterly tactician Tirpitz, endeavouring to convince Hitler that there was no danger in expanding the fleet and that it could even be a desirable element for his continental policy.

If Raeder did not actually win Hitler over to the Navy's 'cause', he nevertheless seems to have convinced him of the fleet's usefulness as a political instrument. At any rate speeches which Hitler made subsequently in Kiel and Wilhelmshaven indicate that he had revised his original position.[11] Thus in September 1933 speaking before a gathering of naval officers, Raeder was able to state that 'the Reich Chancellor himself continually mentions the necessity of expanding the fleet and is firmly convinced of the Navy's great importance, not least as a influential factor in international affairs'.[12] The direct contact which Raeder had thus skilfully established with Hitler (there is no evidence that Hammerstein or Fritsch enjoyed comparable contact) was to have both beneficial and undesirable effects on the Navy at every level.

Now increasingly indifferent to foreign policy considerations, armaments policy had a stimulating effect on the Navy leadership in late 1933. This was evident in the Replacement Shipbuilding Programme of March 1934 which Raeder decided was to disregard international ties in order that exclusively German interests could be served. With the proposed building of 8 battleships, 3 aircraft carriers, 18 cruisers, 48 destroyers and a total of 72 submarines to be completed by 1949,[13] this programme now exceeded the size of the 'Versailles fleet'. Not only the tonnage of the individual types of ship as Raeder had explained to Hitler the year before but also the numerical size of the future fleet had been chosen solely with Germany's particular needs in mind.[14]

Continual disagreement on the extent to which the ships were to be armed, on when their construction should commence and on other planning details obscure the programme's more fundamental significance. Leaving aside details the real question can be asked as to what military – political aims lay behind the shipbuilding plans of March 1934. A first indication of these may be taken from Admiral von Freyberg-Eisenberg-Allmendingen, the Navy's representative of long standing at the disarmament conference in Geneva. In early February 1934 he told a representative of the Foreign Ministry that the Navy was thinking in terms of 'parity' with France.[15] This was a more or less logical conclusion drawn from numerous manoeuvres since 1925/6 testing the conditions governing naval warfare as part of a European war on several fronts against France and one of her east-European allies above all Poland.[16] In mid-February 1934 the

Head of the operational section of the Naval Command, Rear Admiral Groos, reformulated the principle of 'parity' as applied to the implementation of the shipbuilding programme in precise terms: '(1) qualitative equality of status (*Gleichberechtigung*), (2) quantitative equality with France and Italy and (3) a short transitional phase leading to the restoration of equality'.[17] And going beyond the March plan, Raeder sent a directive at the end of May/beginning of June 1934 to all administrative departments concerned, which stated that 'the size of the fleet is to be fixed at a ratio of 33⅓ per cent of the British tonnage'.[18] This figure was later changed to 35 per cent which according to the Washington Agreement of 1922 corresponded exactly to the principle of 'parity' with France.[19] Experts in the Navy leadership came to the conclusion however that the 35 per cent figure did not ensure parity with France especially regarding cruisers.[20] Following this, Groos demanded: 'A different ratio must therefore be selected for cruisers, destroyers and submarines'. Consequently Raeder gave the order to make a figure of 50 per cent the basis of further calculations. This led in mid-June to a satisfactory result; the principle of parity with France was guaranteed by a ratio of naval strength in relation to the British fleet of 2 : 1.

In the event of conflict, 'parity' was not only intended to prevent the French fleet from penetrating the Baltic but also to disrupt French shipping lanes in the Atlantic[21] and if possible in the Mediterranean by naval engagements; that is in areas of crucial importance to Great Britain and with a fleet still only half the strength of its British counterpart. The target of parity was examined and decided upon in a specific political situation. The Reich had withdrawn from the League of Nations' system of collective security. It was moreover embarking on a large-scale process of army armament and was about to create an air force which would threaten the security of France and Britain. And yet despite this the Navy leaders officially held to their belief that an understanding with Britain was the precondition of any naval policy and especially that of parity!

One is quite justified in doubting the official phraseology and must recall the strong anti-British thinking of the Tirpitz school within the Navy and the long-term nature of the naval armaments programme. According to the Replacement Ship-building Programme of 1934, the fleet was to be ready in 15 years time at the earliest! Given such circumstances was it not, in fact, a natural requirement, indeed a bitter necessity, to avoid any conflict with the foremost naval power, Great Britain, and to advocate every possibility for a political understanding at least during the initial phase in the construction of the German fleet? Like Tirpitz whose heir he regarded himself to be, Raeder was well able to distinguish between the political necessities of the day and the long-term consequences of assembling a fleet.

One example of this is provided by discussions held in late June 1934 at which Raeder presented the proposals for the construction of the fleet, which had been worked out since March, to Hitler, Neurath and Blomberg.[22] Again, parity with France was to the fore, and it can be reasonably assumed that the Head of the Naval Command spoke strongly in favour of the 50 per cent solution worked out a few days previously by his office. A decision was not forthcoming, however, and it says much for Raeder's tenacity and identification with the optimum programme that only a few days later, on 27 June, he used the return from abroad of the commander of the light cruiser *Karlsruhe* as an opportunity of once more discussing basic problems with Hitler.[23] He did in fact obtain something of a decision, namely a dramatic increase in the tonnage of the battleships 'D' and 'E' already on order, as well as an increase in their armament strength.

The decisive question of further armaments planning lies concealed in one line of Raeder's abbreviated notes: 'Entwicklung Fl. später ev. gegen E. . . . Tradition hochhalten. Ich: von 1936 an gr. Schiffe mit 35cm. Wenn Geld ja. Bündnis 1899. Lage 1914?' They might be translated thus: 'Development fl[eet]. later poss[ibly]. against E[ngland].' and 'keep up tradition. Me: from 1936 on, lge. ships with 35cm. If money yes. Alliance 1899. Situation 1914?' There has been a great deal of speculation as to the meaning of this line because it does not fit into the picture of naval armament in the Third Reich which has emerged from memoirs and historical interpretations. If one considers this passage in conjunction with demands for parity with France, which the Naval Command had been working intensively towards for months, and their ramifications for relations with Britain, then there can be no doubt that Raeder here openly mentioned to Hitler the consequences of his naval policy. Raeder was of course banking on a long and peaceful development since the building of the fleet was only conceivable on a long-term basis. But – and this may well have been how Raeder reasoned – would an alliance with Britain in 1899 have prevented the First World War? Since he belonged to the Tirpitz school his answer to this question had to be 'no'. Therefore steps would have to be taken to make sure that the fleet would possibly be able to be used against Britain later, 'with a good chance of success' to use Beck's phrase: hence parity with France, and hence large ships with 35cm guns as soon as possible. Raeder, of course, kept his vision to himself; for the time being it did not form a topic of conversation within the naval leadership; Hitler however was no Wilhelm II; he had his own ideas and treated the Navy with detachment as just one of the many instruments of power at his disposal. In his skilful efforts to secure and promote the Navy's interests by his direct contact with Hitler, Raeder failed to appreciate the fundamental contradiction between his own necessarily long-term armaments planning and Hitler's political decisions based on short-term tactical considerations. This explains the Navy's rude awakening when Hitler turned against Britain at a moment which it regarded as far too premature.

The further development of the Navy's armaments planning was determined by the naval agreement signed with Great Britain in June 1935. On the German side, from the outset, tactical considerations stood in the forefront of the negotiations[24] which had commenced on 27 November 1934 when Hitler broached the subject with Ambassador Phipps. For Hitler any break in Germany's isolation on an international level was an advantage in view of the decisions on army and air force armament to be taken early in 1935 after the return of the Saar to the Reich. The results of such decisions would be impossible to conceal. In contrast the programmatic aspects of Hitler's policy towards Britain together with the specific time schedule attached to the planning and construction of the fleet allowed temporary compromises. The view Hitler repeatedly expressed in the course of the discussions, to the effect that the German fleet's main task lay in the Baltic, was of a purely tactical nature given the decisions[25] on shipbuilding taken up to that point. The naval leadership's thoughts also concurred here. On the one hand Raeder took every opportunity of emphasising to the British that the build-up of the German fleet was in no way directed against Great Britain. On the other hand however he pressed for 'as short a duration of the agreement as possible (circa 5 years) . . . especially since we can reach 35 per cent of the British tonnage in considerably less than 10 years'.[26] The emphasis Hitler placed on the fact that the relative size of 35 per cent was a 'final' figure had no validity within the Navy. The Anglo-German naval agreement in no way amounted to a 'renunciation' by the Navy of its longer-range aims. The political as well as the military leadership saw it not as a permanent but as a temporary settlement of the balance of Anglo-German naval power. 'The agreement of 1935 was thus merely a concealment, a diplomatic deception, and thus satisfied both Hitler's foreign policy requirements as well as Raeder's ideas on the future of the German Navy'.[27] It was moreover decisive that in the course of preparatory discussions in the years 1934/5 Raeder became certain that the direction of Hitler's continental policy was in complete accord with the Navy's traditional ultimate goal, expressed in the phrase 'parity with France'.

The more the decisions ratified as early as winter 1934/5 began to have their effect and the more the basic 'temporary nature' of the Anglo-German naval agreement was reflected in planning and actual armaments measures, the less the question of future relations with Great Britain could be avoided. The taboo which since the First World War had surrounded the subject of renewed conflict with British sea power had to give way. Yet, at this point, no new definition of aims was worked out as this would have meant facing up to the possibility of the impossible, namely conflict with Great Britain.

In the Navy's operational planning this taboo was accompanied by the unquestioned belief in Britain's benevolent neutrality in the event of a European war on several fronts. The fact that the cohesive effects this belief had within the Navy recognisably waned as early as 1936 is not without significance and is characteristic of the new developments taking place within the Navy. On the one hand the 'Provisional Battle Orders for the Navy'[28] of May 1936 explicitly ruled out any conflict with Great Britain. And even in February 1937 in a talk given to Hitler, Blomberg, Neurath and several Party officials, Raeder speaking on the subject of naval warfare on the open sea proceeded from the basic premise of Britain's benevolent neutrality.[29] In autumn 1936, on the other hand, doubts began to be expressed within the Navy leadership, regarding this, the premise of all previous planning,[30] particularly in connection with the German intervention in Spain. Raeder himself stressed the question of overseas naval bases in a way hardly compatible with the hypothesis of British neutrality. Finally in summer 1937 the question of conducting a naval war against Britain was fully discussed among

Navy leaders on the basis of a study by Commander Heye on the
'Tasks of Naval Warfare 1937/8'.[31] The anti-British element of the
German naval tradition, a legacy of the Tirpitz era, came
increasingly to the fore and prepared the ground within the Navy
for the open change of attitude towards Britain. This was finally
manifested at a political level by the so-called 'Hoßbach' conference of 5 November 1937 at which Hitler outlined his expansionist programme for the coming years, and the consequences of the
crisis of May 1938.[32] After the uncertainties of previous years this
also gave naval planning a new objective of wider scope.

At the conference on 5 November 1937 called by Hitler and
attended by the heads of the *Wehrmacht* and Foreign Minister von
Neurath, Raeder according to Colonel Hoßbach's account made
no comment on the policy Hitler announced of settling the 'German
question' by force beginning in 1943–5 at the latest. Nor did the
Commander-in-Chief of the Navy join with Blomberg and Fritsch
in their opposition to the views Hitler expressed on the expected
French and British reaction to any German move against Austria
and Czechoslovakia. Instead he was interested in the debate, on the
agenda for the second half of the meeting (not recorded by
Hoßbach), on the decisions regarding the continuation of rearmament. Here Raeder was able to carry his demands through
successfully and in full.[33]

Raeder was able to interpret the picture Hitler painted of the
European power situation, the aims he announced and his suggested solutions as an endorsement of the course his own policy on
the fleet had taken up to that point. Hitler had recognised the
impossibility of attaining economic autarky within the foreseeable
future: the Reich would remain dependent on overseas imports, the
protection of which was the Navy's traditional and undisputed task.
Hitler's preoccupation with Britain's reaction to any German
expansion in eastern central Europe as well as the Army's
concurrence on this particular point strengthened Raeder in his
belief expressed since 1934 that the fleet would later possibly have to
be used against Britain. Although Hitler repeatedly gave his
assurance that he was proceeding on the assumption that Britain
would not intervene in a conflict between the Reich and
Czechoslovakia and Austria, he could not exclude the possibility
altogether. Despite the fact that his overall conception was still
directed in the main towards the Continent, this gradual change in
in Hitler's stance to a more and more openly anti-British position

was obviously of great significance for Raeder. The anti-British component which had long been a part of his policy was now shared and confirmed by the Reich Chancellor who accepted political responsibility for it.

That it took more than four years for it to be realised that the demand for parity with France and the concomitant operations planning entailed unavoidable political and strategic confrontation with Britain can, in the final analysis, only be explained in psychological terms. Just as the traumatic events of November 1918 dominated Naval thinking until well after the Second World War,[34] so the maxim of excluding Britain on principle from all possible coalitions directed against the Reich – a product of the experiences of the Tirpitz era, the First World War and the Navy's weakness – also prevented their comprehending what the consequences of their own actions must be. Raeder although in no doubt as to the temporary nature of this maxim was nevertheless himself one of the prime examples of this thinking. The tight hold that autistic thinking had taken in the Navy is revealed by the fact that it was fully half a year after the conference of 5 November 1937, at which conflict with Great Britain had first been discussed as a realistic possibility, before Raeder openly made the fact known to a larger circle of Navy officers.[35] Nevertheless it took external events to bring the Navy leadership round to a realisation of the consequences of the incorrect assumptions which had lain behind the whole of naval armament planning since 1934/5.

In June 1938, in connection with the crisis which resulted from the partial mobilisation of the Czech forces on 20/21 May 1938 and Hitler's conference with the heads of the *Wehrmacht* on 28 May,[36] Raeder ordered Commander Heye of the operational section of the Naval Command to prepare a memorandum on the possibility of 'waging a naval war against Britain and the resultant requirements in terms of strategic objectives and the build-up of the Navy'.[37] The first draft of the memorandum was ready in August. Commander Heye proceeded from the assumption that in a war with Great Britain, Germany would not be able to maintain her own overseas imports and that the Navy would not be of sufficient strength to break any British blockade. Thus the aim of naval warfare could only be the persistent disruption of British overseas trade. This definition of strategic aims would in turn affect the types of ship chosen for the fleet. Heye and Vice-Admiral Guse, Chief of the operational section of the Naval Command, advocated that priority be given to the building of fast battleships with a long operational range, small cruisers and submarines which corresponded to the type of 'cruiser warfare' they favoured. The memorandum's weakness is apparent on the question of how this 'cruiser warfare' on the open sea was to be supported and supplied from Germany given her geographical position. Even if, at the outbreak of war, all the ships necessary for such a war were out in the Atlantic and if logistics were secured by the existence of supply ships, this particular form of economic war would be over in three months at the most. To come some way towards solving the problem, Heye recommended either the acquisition of overseas bases or the extension of Germany's coastal base to include the whole French Channel coast as far as Brest.

Raeder offered the Fleet Commander, Admiral Carls, and his successor, Admiral Boehm, the opportunity to comment. They also agreed with the basic contention of Heye's memorandum and put forward individual suggestions which helped make more concrete the proposals for the types of ship the future fleet was to comprise.[38] Furthermore, Carls used the occasion to give expression to the idea, nurtured in naval circles since the turn of the century, of Germany as a world power based on naval supremacy:

> If Germany, according to the will of the Führer, is to attain a secure *position of world power*, then besides sufficient colonial possessions, she needs *secure sea routes and secure access to the open sea*...War against Britain means, at the same time, war against the Empire, against France, and possibly also against Russia and a whole succession of countries overseas, in other words, against one half to two-thirds of the countries of the world.

The Fleet Commander did not leave it at this grandiose vision however; he believed he could show a way to achieve this goal. He demanded that the French, Dutch and Danish coasts be occupied in order to extend the Navy's coastal operational base. Besides the speedy build-up of a strong home fleet which would operate on the seas as far away as the western coastal waters of the British Isles, he suggested an overseas fleet, consisting of four combat groupings each with one battle cruiser, one heavy cruiser and aircraft carrier as well as destroyers, submarines and logistics vessels, which was to operate independently on the open seas. This certainly was an alternative to the comparatively modest ideas Heye had in mind:

but what an alternative! Such utter lack of realism and such hubris on the part of a responsible military leader is to say the least astonishing. The Fleet Commander's ideas show dramatically that the Tirpitzian tradition continued unbroken. They betray a mentality that still regarded the demand for parity with France or the 35 per cent settlement of the Anglo-German naval agreement as purely temporary expedients; a mentality whose avowedly shocked reaction to Germany's open change to an attitude of hostility towards Britain early in 1938 was not so much caused by the action itself as by the fact that it came at an unfavourable time for the Navy in the armaments sphere.

What was the relationship between the broad scope of the objectives of naval policy and the results of armament after 1933? The increase in personnel proceeded relatively smoothly.[39] From around 15,000 officers, non-commissioned officers and men in November 1932, the number had risen to 78,305 by the outbreak of war; that is the navy had grown to five times its earlier personnel strength. The Navy's officer corps numbered 1100 in November 1932, 1604 on 1 November 1935, and 4405 officers of all grades by 1 October 1939.

A clear picture of developments is given by the budget for the build-up of the Navy (in million Reichsmark),[40] as shown in Table 5.1. The 1939 budget exceeded that of 1932 more than twelve times. The pre-First World War Fleet construction under Tirpitz was put firmly in the shade by such rates of increase. It is interesting to note from the table that the percentage of the budget allocated to the building of ships falls steadily after 1936.

By the end of 1937 the situation regarding ships had improved compared to early 1933 in that now the ships at the Navy's disposal were almost exclusively modern warships, although the total

TABLE 5.1

	Shipbuilding	*Percentage*	*Total budget*
1932	49.6	26.4	187.4
1933	76.1	24.5	311.8
1934	172.3	34.7	496.5
1935	287.0	41.3	695.1
1936	561.3	48.4	1160.7
1937	603.1	40.8	1478.5
1938	458.8	26.1	1756.3
1939	545.1	22.8	2389.9

number of vessels had decreased with the increased size of the individual ships.[41] The fleet now had 3 battleships, 6 light cruisers, 7 destroyers, 12 torpedo boats and 36 submarines. In addition construction orders had been placed by this time for 4 battleships (the *Scharnhorst, Gneisenau, Bismarck* and *Tirpitz*), 2 aircraft carriers, 5 heavy cruisers (the *Blücher, Hipper, Prinz Eugen, Seydlitz* and *Lützow*), 15 destroyers, 18 torpedo boats and 36 submarines. Of these, 2 battleships (the *Scharnhorst* and *Gneisenau*), one heavy cruiser (the *Hipper*), 14 destroyers and 21 submarines were in service by the outbreak of war.

The picture is rounded off when one realises that the orders for the *Scharnhorst* and the *Gneisenau* had already been placed in January 1934, those for the two aircraft carriers in November 1935 and for the *Hipper* in October 1934. The length of time taken to build the two battleships was due first and foremost to the fact that the original order was for two pocket battleships and that uncertainty as to their strength of armament continued to exist even after the plans were finally changed. The delays were also attributable to the fact that the German ship-yards were for the first time in years confronted with the specific problems of building warships as well as with the time-consuming need to gain experience. Moreover, the negative effects of the acceleration of armament, repeatedly demanded by Hitler, began to be felt for the first time in 1935. The Navy leadership made the following statement:[42]

> It is not possible to accelerate the construction of battleships, cruisers, destroyers, fleet escort vessels, torpedo boats, mine sweepers and aircraft carriers since the quickest possible schedules have already been set, the ship-yards are working at the limits of their capacity and all available skilled workers are fully employed. . . . The German ship-yards can accept no new orders for the time being.

The scope and speed attained in fleet construction since 1933, as well as its resultant problems, could not be better expressed.

It was of decisive importance, however, that the reorientation of Navy planning involved in the new attitude towards Great Britain happened at a time when concrete armaments programmes and those of shipbuilding in particular, were being increasingly affected by the crisis which was evident in the German armaments industry.[43] Besides technical difficulties and the lack of skilled workers, which was increasingly making itself felt, it was primarily the short supply of steel and non-ferrous metals to the ship-yards which caused the continual widening of the gap between the objectives set by planning and its results. The dimensions which the general crisis within the shipbuilding industry had already reached are revealed in a report written for Raeder on construction delays which occurred between March and August 1937 on which work had already begun.[44] Going by the completion schedule valid in March 1937, delays of up to 8 months on the large ships and as much as a whole year on aircraft carrier 'A' were calculated. In December 1937 the delays to be expected on all types of ship including torpedo boats ranged from 3 to 22 months, the average figure lying somewhere over rather than under 12 months. It may be seen as characteristic of this strained situation that not one order for one of the larger warships, nor even for a destroyer, was placed during 1937. Given this situation any extension or acceleration of the construction programme as envisaged in the planning of 1937[45] had to be regarded as illusory. It is one of the unique aspects of developments in naval policy under Admiral Raeder that the unsatisfactory results of armament and its increasing economic problems at no time led to an alteration or correction of Naval Planning objectives. On the contrary, the gulf between the existing situation and projections for the future continued to widen.

Since Raeder kept rigidly to his naval policy, the struggle to obtain the requisite quantities of steel and copper and an adequate supply for the ship-yards of the special sheet metal required for the construction of submarines became of paramount importance to him. As a result of the conference of 5 November 1937 he did in fact secure a monthly quota of 74,000 tonnes of steel. Clearly, however, the ship-yards were in no position to make use of this quantity. For April and May 1938 the Navy demanded only 53,000 tonnes, and at 71,000 tonnes in June, the Navy was still using less than the minimum amount it had itself previously calculated as necessary.[46]

It is against this background that one should consider the ideas and plans for a fleet directed against Britain which, following Heye's memorandum, were brought to the attention of the Navy's Commander-in-Chief on 31 October 1938. A plan for a 'temporary objective' had been agreed upon which envisaged a fleet of 10 battleships, 15 fast battleships, 5 heavy, 24 light and 36 small cruisers, 8 aircraft carriers and 249 submarines.[47] Only in very few cases had the possibility of building these new ships by 1942/3 been examined. According to Hitler's thinking in late May 1938, however, on which overall planning considerations were based, he wished in particular to see concrete armaments measures speeded up. Hitler did not want plans, he wanted ships.

During the months of November and December 1938 and January 1939 Raeder gave several verbal reports to Hitler to try to win his approval for the new and extensively modified shipbuilding programme. In opposition to these plans, Hitler persisted in his wish to speed up construction, especially of the battleships, refusing to allow himself to be diverted, even by Raeder offering his resignation.[48] In mid-January 1939 he ordered that 6 battleships be built by 1944. However Raeder did manage to get Hitler on 27 January 1939 to give naval armament priority 'over all other Reich and export orders',[49] so that naval armament received a tremendous boost in 1939. But the building of battleships which was from now on pursued by all possible means, no longer corresponded to the concept, approved by Raeder, of a naval war against Great Britain. Moreover it became apparent in summer 1939 that the directive of 27 January had brought the Navy only short-term success in its competition for its share of raw materials. Thus here too the implementation of the armaments programme, be it short- or long-term, necessarily found itself in difficulties.

When Britain declared war on Germany on 3 September 1939 Raeder summed up the Navy's six-year-plus armament phase thus:[50]

As far as the Navy is concerned, it is obviously not nearly sufficiently armed in autumn 1939 for the great conflict with Britain . . . the surface naval forces are still so far behind the British fleet in terms of numbers and strength that – even at full stretch – they could only demonstrate their readiness to die honourably and thus pave the way for a new fleet.

The tone of resignation apparent in the words of the Navy's Commander-in-Chief reflected the results of an armaments policy which had suffered from the gap between the necessarily long-term nature of the construction work and the short-term nature of political decisions. For example the last naval staff studies before the war, in February/March 1939, were designed to test the conditions and viability of a naval war against Britain beginning *in 1943*. Despite the relatively improved armaments situation the outlook for the Axis Powers was viewed pessimistically.[51] Yet only a few weeks later these opinions were completely overtaken by events: the 'liquidation' of the remainder of the Czech State, Hitler's directive for the attack against Poland and finally Britain's guarantee to Poland. The crucial problem these events posed was aggravated by the lack of clarity in the Navy's strategic objectives which had long suffered from internal contradictions caused by the decay of the Imperial Navy in the First World War. Raeder was constantly aware of the Navy's weakness in relation to the other two services. Like Tirpitz he had attempted to counteract this by establishing direct contact with the leaders of the Republic and later the Third Reich. By doing this he gained for the Navy a relatively special position which in his view was justified by its considerable significance as a political instrument. On the other hand he was not able to prevent Hitler's own decisions from increasingly determining the nature of the military programme for the build-up of the fleet. What is more, the differing expectations as to the duration of a future war (Raeder expected a long economic struggle while Hitler on the contrary expected a *Blitzkrieg*-style war) had a necessarily damaging effect on the Navy.

The lack of realism of the shipbuilding programme of late 1938, its distortion by Hitler's decision of January 1939 taken for political reasons as well as finally the collapse of the ambitious project in September 1939 as a consequence of Great Britain's declaration of war show the extent of the failure of the naval rearmament effort. Raeder's comments[52] dated 3 September 1939 which hark back to the motives behind the final naval assault of the First World War planned for October 1918 reveal how deeply conscious the Navy's Commander-in-Chief was of the failure of his political and strategic aims as well as his own military ambitions.

6 The *Wehrmacht* at the Outbreak of War

In the early hours of the morning of 1 September 1939 German troops marched into Poland. By the end of the month Poland had been defeated. This seemed to confirm the judgement of foreign experts as to the strength and offensive capacity of the *Wehrmacht*, whose six and a half year period of armament had been without precedent. In extensive operations German Army units had engaged and eliminated the enemy. The armoured divisions in particular had completely fulfilled expectations placed in them. Within the first few days of the war the *Luftwaffe* succeeded in destroying the bulk of the Polish air force. Consequently the *Luftwaffe*, now in complete command of the air, was able to give effective support to the Army's military operations. In April 1940, a few months after Poland's defeat, the three services occupied Denmark and Norway in a combined operation which relied heavily on the Navy. The western offensive against the Netherlands, Belgium and France followed only one month later. Daring airborne operations, the massive use of the *Luftwaffe* and the precisely planned deployment of independent armoured divisions with a wide operational range were the main reasons for Germany's success, not only in defeating the Dutch army, forcing the King of Belgium to capitulate and capturing large sections of the French army, but also in driving the British Expeditionary Force from the Continent. The campaign ended after only six weeks in a triumphant victory for German arms with the signing of the armistice with France at Compiègne.[1] Only one year after the outbreak of war the area controlled by the Axis Powers stretched from the North Cape to Sicily and from Brest Litovsk to the west coast of France. Great Britain, now, alone was exposed to the threat of direct attack from Germany. Preparations for the invasion of the island operation 'Sea-lion', and the Battle of Britain were in full swing.

These military successes would seem to permit only one conclusion: that the expansion of the *Wehrmacht* and its provision with
arms, equipment and ammunition had fully measured up to the
requirements of a European war on several fronts. In contrast to the
experiences of the long, bitter and bloody struggle of the First World
War, the overwhelming victory, over France in particular, seemed
to be convincing proof that the *Wehrmacht* was a highly modernised,
efficient military machine with ample reserves of strength which, as
such, must consequently have been the product of meticulous and
intensive planning with specific goals in mind. This picture seems to
a great extent to be contradicted by the findings of the previous
chapters dealing with the armaments programmes of the various
services.[2] According to these, military success seems not to have
been at all carefully planned in advance. Rather one gains the
impression that plans were dominated by an unbridled drive to
expand the services which gradually, but with increasing speed, lost
touch with reality. Military results could not long remain unaffected by this.

Within the Army, the years 1937–9 had been marked by the
attempt to realise in stages the objectives of the 1936 August
armaments programme despite the economic difficulties involved.
As early as November 1936 the Head of the Army Ordnance Office
had to notify his Commander-in-Chief that only half of the Army's
copper requirements could be met.[3] The resulting rationing of non-
ferrous metals introduced on 1 January 1937 bore all the signs of
being merely a way of regulating the shortage but did nothing to
help meet the Army's planned requirements. Thus for example on
10 February 1939 the Army's Commander-in-Chief reported to
Hitler that, because the required copper was not available, a large
proportion of the shells to be manufactured in 1939 would 'for the
time being, be delivered without rotating bands or detonators'.[4] As
a result of the worsening armaments situation it became clear that
the date of 1 October 1939 set by Fritsch for the completion of the
programme could not be adhered to. As early as the beginning of
1937 the General Army Office had come to the conclusion that the
bulk of the peacetime and field army conceived in August 1936
could only be set up by April 1941 at the earliest, thus forecasting
another one and a half year's delay.[5] Only a few weeks after the
conference of 5 November 1937 recorded in Hoßbach's minutes,
which was also concerned with the problems of the armaments
economy, the Head of the General Staff, Beck, announced on behalf

of his superior to the Commander-in-Chief of the *Wehrmacht*, Blomberg, that the Army Armaments Programme could be fully realised by 1 April 1943 at the earliest.[6] Beck drew attention to the cuts and changes which would be necessary to achieve this. According to these for example the motorised units could only be set up by winter 1938/9 because of a shortage of vehicles and their operational readiness could only be guaranteed for 1 April 1939. The supplies of some types of ammunition were down to an amount sufficient for only fifteen days' combat. Finally Beck indicated that 'the whole Army' would not 'be operational over the winter of 1938/9' and that 'even later, very considerable cuts' would have to be faced. On the other hand the alterations to the armaments plan still corresponded to the schedule announced by Hitler on 5 November, according to which the question of German *Lebensraum* would have to be solved by 1943/5 at the latest.

Despite Germany's territorial expansion in 1938 as a result of the Austrian *Anschluss* and the annexation of the Sudetenland, the situation regarding armaments shortage was further considerably aggravated.[7] This was partly due to Hitler's order following the crisis of May 1938 to speed up the extension of the western defences and partly to the inflated armaments programmes of the Navy and *Luftwaffe*. In a note of early 1939 the Army High Command ascertained that the field army had no supply of arms and equipment, that of the infantry divisions 34 had only some of the required weapons and equipment, that the reserve forces possessed only 10 per cent of the small arms they required and that the overall munitions supply had sunk to an amount sufficient for only fifteen days' combat.[8] The following passage from the same note reveals how dramatically the situation was assessed and what military–political convictions influenced decision-making.

> The present situation which has resulted from a shortage of steel is to a certain extent comparable with that prior to the World War. At that time the three army corps which would have helped decide the war quickly during its first year were lacking due to parliament's refusal to grant funds. Today the Army is being refused the quantities of steel necessary to equip it with modern offensive weapons. The results could be the same as in 1914.

The occupation of the remainder of Czechoslovakia and the high quality arms, ammunition and other equipment thus acquired made up for this in a fortuitous and extremely satisfactory manner. These acquisitions, which Hitler described in detail in his speech to the Reichstag[9] of 28 April 1939, meant that one of the aims of the August armaments programme, namely the advanced storage of arms and equipment for fifteen infantry divisions, could in fact be achieved. The armoured divisions also profited from the captured material and the further exploitation of Czechoslovakia's production capacity. It was possible to equip three German armoured divisions with Czechoslovakian combat vehicles for the campaign against France.[10]

As it was, the planning figures which the August programme had set for personnel and the number of active units for 1 September 1939 could now be exceeded, although, as before, there were still considerable deficiencies in the equipping and arming of the troops. The planned field army, which was intended to consist of 2.421 million men, had reached a strength of 2.758 million by 1 September 1939. Instead of the intended 44 divisions of the active army, 53 large units – 35 infantry, 3 mountain, 6 armoured and 4 light divisions as well as 4 motorised infantry divisions and 1 cavalry brigade – were available. The number of units which could be mobilised in 1939 (103) was almost identical to that projected in 1936 (102).[11]

The lack of readiness on the part of the *Luftwaffe* and Navy at the outbreak of war as judged against the planning figures was even more obvious than in the case of the Army. For the *Luftwaffe*, the years 1937–9 were marked by stagnating production. This was caused not only by general economic complications but also by the increasing difficulties of guiding the highly complex process of developing, testing and producing modern aircraft.[12] The difficulties caused by these factors were increased by the expansion of military objectives resulting from the change of attitude to Great Britain and the *Luftwaffe* leadership's consequent enormous armaments programme of autumn 1938. It envisaged the enlargement of the *Luftwaffe* to approximately 19,000 front-line and reserve aircraft as well as 500 ship-borne and transport aircraft by early 1942.[13] This programme of course changed nothing as far as the problems of materials were concerned. In order to maintain the combat-readiness of the Air Force in the event of war, it foresaw a need for aircraft fuel in such quantities that in 1941 '85 per cent of the existing world production of oil' would have to be imported to fill the requisite storage tanks yet to be constructed.[14] These few details alone show how far the gulf between planning conceptions and actual possibilities for armament was widening at the time.

The extent to which planning intentions also diverged from military realities was revealed by the political crisis concerning Czechoslovakia in autumn 1938 which was to test the war-readiness of the *Luftwaffe*. Reports from flying units and ground staff painted a gloomy picture. There were still not enough fully trained flying crews available and the problems of adapting to a second generation of aircraft models (the Me 109, He 111 and Do 17) had not yet been solved. Above all it was clear that the infrastructure of the flying units (all types of reserves, logistics and especially supplies of spare parts) was still extremely inadequate.[15] Nevertheless, with their increased experience, the *Luftwaffe* leadership was able to effect many improvements in the spheres of training and equipping units and to raise the overall level of combat-readiness. Thus in August 1939, 21 groups existed comprising 302 operational squadrons. Over 90 per cent of the 4093 front-line aircraft available on 1 September 1939 were designated fully and immediately operational.[16] Nevertheless as the 2nd Air Fleet Study under the direction of General Felmy had finally shown in May 1939,[17] from the point of view of both armament and training, the *Luftwaffe* was unprepared for a war against France, her east-European allies *and* Great Britain as well.

The same conclusion was even more valid for the Navy. In view of the number of ships available, it is clear that the comment made by the Navy's Commander-in-Chief on Britain's declaration of war that the Navy was 'as yet completely inadequately armed for the great conflict with Britain'[18] was an accurate representation of the situation. Even if one considers that Germany's modern ships posed a serious threat to the generally older British ones, the extent to which Raeder felt his fleet to be inferior nevertheless becomes even more clear when the number of ships in 1939 is compared with the dimensions of the Z-Plan Fleet intended to combat Great Britain.[19] Calculations made by the Armaments Economy Department of the Naval High Command dated 31 December 1938 reveal the drastically utopian character of the fleet construction programme.[20] According to these calculations the Z-Plan Fleet required 6,000,000 tonnes of fuel oil and 2,000,000 tonnes of diesel oil for mobilisation. In 1938 the total German consumption of mineral oil products was 6,150,000 tonnes of which 2,400,000 were produced at home. The Navy's plans aimed at storing imported fuel (for which tanks with a total capacity of 10,000,000 cubic metres were to be constructed by 1945) together with a larger part of the increased home production so that the existing fleet could engage in a war lasting twelve months. Thus in 1939 the Navy was severely handicapped in this respect. In addition to a shortage of fuel, there were serious technical and conceptual deficiencies in particular weapons systems which considerably reduced the functional capacity of the existing naval forces. One example of this was the so-called Torpedo Crisis of 1939/40.[21]

These brief remarks on the level of Army, Air Force and Navy armament at the outbreak of war emphasise rather than conceal the contradiction between the *Wehrmacht*'s military success during the first year of the war and the actual level of German armament, not to mention the prevalent pessimistic view of the country's readiness for war. To attempt to explain this by suggesting that responsible military leadership would naturally never describe an army's level of equipment and training as sufficient would not do justice to the specific German circumstances. In 1939 the *Wehrmacht* clearly did not yet resemble the army envisaged by the military planners. Nevertheless, although particular shortcomings and gaps in armament were evident, these were concealed by the early successes of the war which astonished even the *Wehrmacht*'s own experts.

One decisive weakness in German military developments after 1933, however, has not yet been dealt with in this study. German rearmament was regarded, especially abroad, as a planned, goal-oriented, unified process. This impression, reinforced by propaganda, helps account in some measure for its political effect. Hitler's declaration to the Reichstag on 1 September 1939 that he himself had 'been working for six years . . . to build up the German *Wehrmacht*'[22] could in view of the extent of his dictatorial powers be taken to confirm the image. However the view of the Army, *Luftwaffe* and Navy armaments programmes contained in the previous chapters has shown that there is no question of there having been a well-planned rearmement of the *Wehrmacht* as a whole. Hitler's expansion of the *Wehrmacht* amounted rather to a fundamentally unco-ordinated expansion of its individual services. An overall rearmament programme for the *Wehrmacht* did not exist. As far as one can judge, decisions on the basic programmes of each of the individual services were made without consulting or taking advice from the other two. The *Wehrmacht* was thus little more than the sum of its three distinct parts. Its command was unable to exert decisive influence either of an economic or of a military nature.

In his speech to the *Reichswehr* Generals on 3 February 1933 Hitler had indicated that the 'most dangerous time' for foreign policy would be the period of the 'build-up of the *Wehrmacht*'.[23] It was to be Blomberg's most urgent task to adapt the services' armaments programmes to this situation and to bring them into line with the realities of the existing financial and economic climate. The *Luftwaffe's* armaments programme of June 1933 appears to have followed these instructions, whereas the decisions of December of that year to build-up a peacetime army of 21 divisions did rather the opposite with its disregard for the material aspects of rearmament.[24] Insurmountable difficulties of co-ordination came to light not only in the planning but also in the implementation of the first stage of rearmament. The ordnance offices of the individual services insisted on directing their own armaments intentions quite independently of each other. Thus economic co-operation on armaments never came about, and industry was confronted with three competing consumers and their requirements.[25]

Opposition to a unified organisation of *Wehrmacht* rearmament came in particular from the newly founded *Luftwaffe*. Secretary of State Milch had worked in close co-operation with the President of the Reichsbank, Schacht, on the financial basis for Air Force armament and on the very successful expansion of the industrial basis for aircraft production. But Milch energetically opposed all attempts by the *Wehrmacht* and Army leadership to interfere here and even succeeded in further extending his own sphere of autonomy. He had the long-term armaments programme of July 1934 approved by Hitler personally. The Commander-in-Chief of the *Wehrmacht* seems, in contrast, to have played a subordinate role.[26]

The Navy, like the *Luftwaffe*, sailed on unimpeded in the lee of these disagreements. It also insisted on the right to carry out its own armaments measures independently. From the outset, Raeder had sought and established personal contact with Hitler in the interests of his own armaments plans. At the end of June 1934, by completely by-passing the *Wehrmacht's* Commander-in-Chief, he extracted from Hitler the decision in favour of considerable changes in the planning of ship construction.[27] One result of this was that Blomberg's attempt, as Commander-in-Chief of the *Wehrmacht*, to organise the unified build-up and extension of the armed forces using the full extent of his power had utterly failed by as early as the autumn of 1934.

At first glance it is tempting to attribute this lack of co-ordination *solely* to the unsolved organisational problems, as already mentioned, within the *Wehrmacht* command and the inadequate organisational powers of the Reich Minister of Defence and the Commander-in-Chief of the *Wehrmacht*.[28] The unsatisfactory pattern of command within the *Wehrmacht* doubtless encouraged the traditional tendencies of the individual services towards autonomy. Yet this ignores a more fundamental question. During Weimar the *Reichswehr* leaders had as a result of discussions on the two armaments programmes and the simultaneous 'Special Programme', come to a realisation that the planning and goal-oriented co-ordination of material armaments measures was a long and costly business. Blomberg himself had taken part in these discussions. This debate from which the Navy characteristically kept its distance had been carried out under the constraints of a particular political situation and limited financial possibilities. These constraints eased a good deal as early as 1933, allowing the military leadership in December of that year to carry out an expansion of the Army without any regard to the state of the armaments economy. Nowhere can one more clearly discern the military leadership's belief that the modern planning of the armaments programmes, based as it was on the experiences of the First World War, was neither a reliable guide nor something which should be extended to all three services. Since the decisions of the military commanders thus failed to give due consideration to the economic basis of armament common to all the services within the *Wehrmacht*, the traditional military preference for the autonomy of the separate services was reinforced. The individual expansion of the services was, thus, not only a result of unsolved organisational problems, but also a consequence of the military leadership's incapacity to take due account of the relationship between the economy and rearmament which had radically altered since the First World War.

The increasing independence of the services was also promoted from another quarter. Reich Defence Minister Groener had written at the beginning of his directive, 'The Tasks of the *Wehrmacht*':[29] 'The tasks set for the armed forces by the responsible political authority are to be the basis for their build-up and employment'. During the Third Reich Hitler was the only person who could issue such political directives. Since rearmament held absolute priority within the framework of Hitler's policy, it can be easily imagined that he could have intervened in favour of co-ordinating *Wehrmacht* rearmament. Apart from occasional and very general comments Hitler, as far as is known, never issued any directive dealing with overall *Wehrmacht* rearmament prior to the war nor any which, by a suggestion to limit objectives, would have necessitated even a loose co-ordination of the armaments measures taken by the individual services. Rather as far as any direct involvement can be ascertained on Hitler's part, decisions on the basic armaments programme seem to have been reached with reference only to those aspects relevant to the individual service concerned. Developments in naval armament are a clear example of this. Moreover Hitler considerably increased the competition between the services, on the one hand by constantly demanding that armament be accelerated and, on the other, by continually setting up new institutions with responsibilities in the field of armament.[30] The fact that existing methods of decision-making on armament in no way changed after Hitler took over the supreme command of the *Wehrmacht* in early February 1938 shows how little the expansion of the individual services was due to unresolved problems in the structure of the *Wehrmacht* command. In fact Hitler's new demands increased the pressure of competition between the services.

One institution which stood for a co-ordinated *Wehrmacht* armament, in contrast to the armaments policies pursued separately by the Army, *Luftwaffe* and Navy, was the Defence Economy Staff under Colonel, later Major-General, Thomas.[31] This section had evolved out of the logistics staff of the Army Ordnance Office, was considerably involved in the creation of the first two armaments programmes and was taken over as a department of the *Wehrmacht* Office in November 1934. Since his transfer to the Army Ordnance Office in 1928, Thomas had made a careful study of the economic aspects of preparing and conducting a war and together with colleagues he attempted to convert into practical measures the lesson learned from the First World War: namely that 'economic war' should be assigned a significance equal to that of traditional 'armed warfare'. If the country's economic resources had in fact become a decisive element in war then they must be wisely dealt with, thorough and effective preparations must be made for their employment should war occur and peacetime armament must be fitted into such an overall system. Thomas and his colleagues repeatedly advocated the adoption of their concept in numerous memoranda and discussions.[32] This was a very ambitious programme given the complexity of economic affairs and the technical problems of industrial production. Yet it was not these practical problems which were responsible for the fact that economic preparations for war and armament were not organised and implemented according to 'defence economy' criteria, but rather the refusal of the separate services to subordinate their own armaments programmes to the authority and instructions of a single *Wehrmacht* administrative department. Thus from the outset the *Wehrmacht*'s Defence Economy Staff was limited to the role of advisor and, where possible, arbitrator. Major-General Thomas's staff never managed to exert any decisive influence on essential decisions regarding armaments. His staff and subordinate officers at a local administrative level represented the interests of the *Wehrmacht* in discussion with the armaments industries. Yet the definition of their sphere of competence in relation to organisations and authorities outside the *Wehrmacht* who were involved in armaments was so vague that the possible effectiveness of the one section which concerned itself with co-ordinating *Wehrmacht* armament must be described as extremely circumscribed.

Even the extension of the Army Ordnance Office's responsibilities to include the development and acquisition of particular armaments items for the other two services did little to alter the fact that *Wehrmacht* armament remained the preserve of the individual services. Occasional conferences involving the three services likewise failed to result in any recognisable efforts at co-ordination.[33] Despite his wide-ranging powers, Blomberg could not push through his ideas against Göring and Raeder and evidently gave up the attempt very early on. The only thing which the three armaments programmes had in common seems to have been Hitler's approval and it has already been shown that no co-ordinating influence came from this quarter.

Thus the extent and structure of *Wehrmacht* rearmament was defined solely by the armament programmes of the individual services. The objectives were in turn governed by differing military concepts of a European war on two or more fronts. Moreover their scale continued to increase as a result of Hitler's continual demands for an acceleration of armament. The only factors which limited this otherwise unrestricted process were the marked shortage of raw materials important for armament which first began to be felt in the second half of 1936, the more general economic problems evident from 1937 onwards and finally the growing financial difficulties after the end of the Mefo Bills early in 1938.[34] Thus German rearmament was not, as was generally believed, a comprehensively planned, systematically organised and centrally directed process. Also Hitler had not, as he claimed in his speech to the Reichstag of 1 September 1939, worked for six years 'to build-up the German *Wehrmacht*'. On the contrary as Reich Chancellor and Commander-in-Chief of the *Wehrmacht*, he had neglected the idea of a unified *Wehrmacht* and promoted the unco-ordinated expansion of the separate services.

An analysis of the results of rearmament up to 1939 does not, therefore, provide a convincing explanation for the German *Wehrmacht*'s triumphant successes during the first year of the war. The question still remains whether the *Wehrmacht* had an operative concept which made success possible despite weaknesses and deficiencies in armament. In this connection one thinks primarily of the tactical thinking of the Army's General Staff in view of the Reich's strategic position in the centre of Europe. The fundamental conviction of Ludwig Beck, the long-standing Chief of the General Staff, may be summed up as being that any war in which Germany might be involved would as a result of the existing set of alliances become a European war on several fronts. In other words this meant that any war, especially one initiated by Germany, would inevitably involve France. In the opinion of Beck and probably the higher ranks of the *Wehrmacht* however, the French Army was still the superior military power despite its noticeable short-comings and the German army would not for years be able to match it in terms of armament and training.[35]

These views were more or less those contained in the 'Directive for the Preparation of the *Wehrmacht* for War' issued on 24 June 1937 by the Reich Defence Minister and the Commander-in-Chief of the *Wehrmacht*.[36] In the general guidelines it established that in view of the general political situation, 'Germany need not think in terms of an attack from any side'. Nor did Germany intend to 'let loose a war on Europe'. Nevertheless, it was necessary that the German *Wehrmacht* be 'constantly at the ready' in order to 'counteract an attack at any time' and to 'take full military advantage of politically promising opportunities'. This last point was supplemented by the order to hasten preparations for a 'secret mobilisation' to enable Germany to 'begin a war with – in terms of its strength and timing – a surprise attack'. The directive described only two probable war situations: the war on two fronts with emphasis on the west (coded 'Red') and the same with emphasis on the south-east ('Green'). In the 'Red' plan the instructions envisaged a purely defensive war against France, the objective of which was the maintenance of the Rhine–Black Forest line against the anticipated French offensive. The 'Green' plan was a variation on this which dealt with the 'hostile attitude' of Czechoslovakia and Russia. Operation 'Green' was based on the intention of forestalling an 'impending attack by a stronger coalition', consisting of France, Czechoslovakia and Russia, 'by a surprise German operation against Czechoslovakia'. It was to be the 'aim and goal of this attack' to 'smash' the Czech armed forces and occupy 'Bohemia and Moravia' in order to remove for 'the duration of the war' the threat posed 'to the western campaign' by an attack from the rear.

Alongside these points, so-called 'special cases' were listed which were to be dealt with and 'carefully thought out' only within the High Commands of the services. Of particular interest is the 'Extended Red/Green Plan', which allowed for a possible deterioration in the military-political situation initially envisaged in plans 'Red' and 'Green', namely if Britain, Poland and Lithuania were individually or together to join the enemy coalition. The new circumstances were described in the directives thus: 'This would worsen our military situation to an intolerable degree, even to the point where there was no hope of victory. The political leadership will thus do everything to maintain the neutrality of these countries, and that of Britain and Poland in particular'.

The basic concept of the directive can be aptly summed up by the term, 'offensively-conducted strategic defence'. Beck himself had used this term before in his major memorandum of 30 December 1935 on 'Increasing the Army's Offensive Capacity'.[37] Thus the directive of June 1937 was in full accord with his operational concepts.

Hitler's declaration[38] at the meeting with Blomberg, von Neurath and the Commanders-in-Chief of the three services on 5 November 1937 altered the initial premises for the *Wehrmacht*'s operations planning in one fundamental respect. The directive of 24 June 1937 proceeded from the old question of how to solve the military problem of a war on two fronts. The political situation was taken to be more or less that defined by the Paris peace treaties. Operative planning definitely contained potentially aggressive elements of a generally revisionist nature. But no clear political objective as yet existed. It was first provided by Hitler's declaration that the 'aim of German policy' was 'to secure the survival of the German nation, and to increase its numbers', that it was therefore a 'question of *Lebensraum*' and that this problem could only be solved by the 'use of force' which was 'never without its risks'. Hitler did not in fact go beyond the territorial goals already mentioned in the directive of June 1937 (Czechoslovakia and Austria) but he nevertheless made it clear that this was only the first step on the way to achieving the total solution at which he aimed. From this point onwards the day to day work of the General Staff was gripped by the dynamism of his political will and was placed increasingly under pressure. The translation of the new political objective into military terms came about on the initiative of the Head of the National Defence Department at the *Wehrmacht* Office, Colonel Jodl, in his directive of 21 December 1937. In it he stated:[39]

> When Germany has achieved full readiness for war in all respects, the military preconditions will have been created for an offensive war against Czechoslovakia, and hence for the solution of the problem of German *Lebensraum* which can be successfully implemented even if one or other of the Great Powers intervenes against us.

This was a very restricted interpretation of Hitler's statement since the latter did not consider that the defeat of Czechoslovakia would offer a definitive solution to the problem of *Lebensraum*. Besides, the phrase, 'full readiness for war in all respects', was open to differing interpretations.

General Ludwig Beck, who in his memorandum of 12 November 1937 had sharply criticised Hitler's intended action against Czechoslovakia and Austria,[40] raised no objections to the directive of 21 December. Any attack on Czechoslovakia must in his view necessarily form part of a European war on several fronts and depended on the *Wehrmacht* being 'fully prepared for war'. This was for him the difference between the December 1937 directive and Blomberg's directive of 2 May 1935, which was intended to stimulate Beck to formulate plans for an isolated 'surprise' attack against Czechoslovakia.[41] Political and military developments during 1938, however, led to the situation where Beck's assessment of the military situation, which had been based on the assumption of a European war on several fronts and which had previously formed the basis of *Wehrmacht* operative planning, was dropped. In March

1938 during military preparations for the annexation of Austria, Beck himself was the first to encounter Hitler's determination to base the timing and methods of military action on his own judgement. The decision in favour of Hitler's suggestion to concentrate on one adversary at a time was reached in summer 1938 in the discussions on the military action against Czechoslovakia. Beck's attempt, by means of the General Staff study tour of 1938, to prove that conflict with Czechoslovakia necessarily implied confrontation with the western powers failed.[42] Contrary to expectations, the study showed that the German Army now seemed capable of breaking through the Czech system of defences and bringing about a decisive resolution of the conflict in a relatively short time. And it was precisely this conclusion on which Hitler had based his assessment of the political situation, namely that neither France nor Britain was in a position, or even willing, to risk a conflict with the Reich on Czechoslovakia's account.[43] The results of the General Staff study tour undermined Beck's military arguments against an isolated action against Czechoslovakia and this was the deeper reason behind his resignation. Developments seemed, politically and militarily, to have overtaken the dogma of the inevitability of a European war on several fronts. The Munich crisis of late September 1938 and the occupation of the remainder of the Czech state in March 1939 were examples of this.

From early 1938 onwards, as a consequence of these developments which were in themselves partly the result of massive rearmament, *Wehrmacht* planning was increasingly guided by Hitler's current, short-term political intentions. The directive of June 1937 had assigned the combined armed forces of the Reich tasks based on specific situations of political conflict and had given the individual services clearly defined orders which fitted into the overall scheme. From this point onwards however its place was taken with conspicuous frequency by directives for individual actions which demanded 'lightning' or 'surprise' attacks or 'coups de main'.[44] The *Wehrmacht* High Command was no longer able to issue an overall 'Directive for the Preparation of the *Wehrmacht* for War'. Even in the case of conflict with France and Britain, separately or together, which according to Hitler was quite likely, there were no directives for the *Wehrmacht* as a whole. This led to the paradox that 'War Directive No. 1' signed by Hitler on 31 August 1939 was more concerned with the less probable event of conflict with the Western powers than with Hitler's war against Poland which, because already dealt with in detailed preparatory studies, was discussed in only two paragraphs.[45]

Thus developments in operations planning studies also fail to account adequately for the military successes of the first year of the war. It is clear that intensive planning for the invasion of Poland and concentration on this one enemy from early 1939 onwards contributed to the rapid and sweeping victory. This was also the case for the campaign in the west, which was likewise preceded by a phase of intensive planning, but not for that against Denmark and Norway. Yet if one considers developments in armament alongside operative planning a much fuller picture emerges. The forced rearmament resulted in a numerically extremely strong army which, despite all its weaknesses and short-comings, was at least in possession of modern equipment. The level of armament attained, although in part extremely limited in terms of supplies and reinforcements available, nevertheless lent the Army a superior offensive strength – albeit of limited duration. Operations planning was adapted to the given armaments situation by concentrating on one particular strategy at a time, be it 'Green' (Czechoslovakia), 'White' (Poland), or 'Red' (France). The so-called *Blitzkrieg* was thus not a coherent operative concept consciously evolved by the military leadership. On the contrary it was much more a reflection of Hitler's political demands and in fact a result of developments which had taken place in the domestic and in particular the armaments economies.[46]

All this already suggests that the successes of the first year of the war were not the result of purely military considerations. The Army, *Luftwaffe* and Navy had indeed created many of the prerequisites for success as has already been illustrated, but their significance can only be fully grasped when seen against the overall framework of German war planning.

In addition one must also bear the simple fact in mind that any military success also depends on the strength and actions of the adversary. In this respect – just to touch upon the problem – the German victories in the east and north were hardly surprising given the superiority of the *Wehrmacht* in numbers and arms. The rapid and total defeat of France, on the contrary, was experienced by the one participant as a shock and by the other as an unexpected and overwhelming triumph. Yet on this particular point a closer examination reveals that the political structure of the French nation at the outbreak of war, the fundamental pacifism which had resulted from the experiences and consequences of the First World War and which broadly permeated almost every social class, together with the state of French armaments, and finally the fortress mentality which held the military in its grip; all these were decisive preconditions for the German success.[47] Hitler had won a victory over opponents who 'were unable or unwilling to resist'.[48] The real test was yet to come.

7 Armaments within the Framework of German War Policy

The previous chapter concluded that in view of the grossly inadequate level of German rearmament in autumn 1939, the unexpected extent of the successes during the first year of the war could not be adequately accounted for solely by a review of military factors. This is even more true of an examination of overall military developments in Germany from 1933 to 1939, which can only be properly understood when viewed as an integral part of Hitler's policies.

Only four days after his appointment as Reich Chancellor, Hitler had described the build-up of the armed forces to the *Reichswehr* leaders as the all-important prerequisite for Germany regaining her status as a great power.[1] The fundamental importance of this declaration becomes apparent when the role played by the use of force, i.e. war, in Hitler's political philosophy and its aims is examined. Only against such a background can one discern the true proportions of the military problems of planning and implementing *Wehrmacht* armament which have formed the focus of this study. For however self-evident it might seem the fact still has to be stated: without Hitler the rearmament of the *Wehrmacht* would have followed quite a different course.

Although the individual elements of Hitler's world view seem so heterogeneous and full of contradictions, his Social Darwinist belief that 'struggle in all its forms' governed not only the life of the individual but also the development of individual nations may be viewed alongside his racial theories as determining the basis and scope of his political decisions.[2] This ideology, according to which peace was regarded merely as a preparation for war and alliances were only to be evaluated for their relevance for a future war,[3] formed the basis for Hitler's ideas on foreign policy, the nucleus of which was the acquisition of new living space (*Lebensraum*) in the east. Hitler formulated these principles in his 'Second Book' in 1928.[4] The first chapter entitled 'War and Peace in the Struggle for Survival (*Lebenskampf*)' begins as follows:

> Politics is history in the making. History itself represents the course of a nation's struggle for survival. I use the word *Lebenskampf* intentionally because the truth is that every struggle for one's daily bread, whether in peace or in war, is an eternal struggle against thousand upon thousand of obstacles, just as life itself is an eternal struggle against death.[5]

He continues:

> What is valid for individuals is also valid for nations. . . . But if politics is history in the making and history itself represents the struggle of individuals and nations for self-preservation and survival, the politics is in effect the carrying out of a nation's struggle for survival. . . . Thus politics is the leader in the struggle for survival – the guide and organiser – and its effectiveness, quite independently of how man describes it formally, will determine the decision on the life or death of a nation.[6]

The nations' struggle for survival was seen as taking place on the 'surface of a globe of finite size. . . . The drive behind the struggle for survival' was seen as resulting from 'restricted living space'.[7] Germany's aim must be to turn away 'from all endeavours in the sphere of international industry and trade' and instead to concentrate 'all [its] strength . . . in order to show our nation the way to survival by giving it adequate living space for the next hundred years'. Hitler concluded with the explanation that living space could only 'be found in the east' and that this goal depended 'for its realisation on extensive military means'.[8]

When in power Hitler held firmly to these ideological premises in his policies. This was to have important consequences for the fundamental orientation and practical aims of domestic, economic and foreign policy.[9]

According to Hitler, domestic policy was the 'art of securing for a nation the strength, in the shape of racial quality and numbers, necessary to secure living space'.[10] In more concrete terms he announced to the *Reichswehr* commanders on 3 February 1933 that his goal was to achieve 'a complete transformation in the present domestic political situation' in Germany. There was to be

> no toleration of any opinions which oppose the goal (e.g. pacifism)! Those holding to such views must be crushed. Marxism to be completely eradicated. Youth, and the people as a whole, to be recruited to the belief that only a struggle can save us and that everything must make way for this belief. . . . Strict authoritarian government. Removal of the cancer of democracy![11]

In relinquishing the *Reichswehr*'s function to maintain order in the State, as was revealed to the cabinet on 30 January 1933, Blomberg the new Reich Defence Minister had contributed to the ease with which Hitler and his Party were able during the months that followed to carry out their programme without encountering opposition of any consequence. This programme corresponded completely with prevailing views within the higher officer corps, although individual officers did, of course, have reservations.[12] The crushing of the socialist parties and trade unions, the self-dissolution of the bourgeois parties and *Gleichschaltung* in almost every area of public life hardly affected the *Reichswehr* leaders at all. On the contrary, they endeavoured to do everything in their power to influence the 'rearming' (*Wiederwehrhaftmachung*) of the nation, and its youth in particular, as called for by Hitler. It was on this level above all that the conflict with Röhm and the SA developed which Hitler decided in the *Reichswehr*'s favour.

As later on in the conflict with Himmler's SS, the *Reichswehr* leadership was guided less by political motives and more by the desire to maintain at all costs the position of the *Reichswehr* or the *Wehrmacht* as 'the nation's sole armed power [*Waffenträger*]'.[13] What ultimately determined their action was the view that Hitler's domestic political programme seemed for the first time, and to a considerable degree, to present the opportunity of acting on the military lessons learned from the First World War. The war had taught that future wars, as violent conflicts between industrialised countries, necessitated the rigorous preparation and organisation of the nation and its personnel and material resources for war, even during periods of peace. Hitler's 'strict authoritarian government', which was the general direction taken in domestic policy, seemed to the military to create the necessary climate for such preparations.

Early in 1933 in view of the total of six million unemployed, such considerations seemed to be academic. On 1 February Hitler had of course proclaimed that the intention behind his economic policy was 'to save the German farmer' and 'to save the German worker by a strong and thorough attack on unemployment'. He had, however, said nothing on the details of how this was to be accomplished.[14] Speaking before the *Reichswehr* commanders on 3 February he regarded 'radical change' in the economic situation in the near future as unlikely, 'since the German nation's living space was too small'. He was convinced 'that the present economic situation could only be altered by political power and struggle' and described the goal, in his view also associated with the solution of the Reich's economic problems, in no uncertain terms as: 'The conquest and ruthless Germanisation of new living space in the east'. Finally in the cabinet sitting of 8 February, the Chancellor demanded that all measures concerned with creating employment should be taken in close conjunction with the idea of 'rearming' the nation,[15] i.e. with rearmament itself. Hitler held firmly to this principle throughout the following years and did in fact regard the economy purely as an instrument for creating the conditions necessary for his expansionist policy. In Schacht, the President of the Reichsbank, Hitler found an expert who by means of the Mefo Bills created the financial basis for the services' first rearmaments programmes and who also with his 'New Plan' brought the corpus of economic policy into line with overall political strategy. When this system broke down as early as 1935/6 as a result of the rapidly growing demands of the services' armaments programmes, the National Socialist leadership, and Hitler and Göring in particular, reacted with the announcement of economic mobilisation in the shape of the Four-Year Plan. At the conclusion of his memorandum of August 1936, Hitler demanded in short that the *Wehrmacht* should be 'operational' in four years and that the economy was after the same period to be 'ready for war'.[16]

It is not surprising that the military leadership agreed with this use of the economy as expressed in Hitler's words and actions and made great efforts to work towards it in the day-to-day process of rearmament as well. The officers who since 1927 had worked out the armaments programmes were quite aware that it was not the number of weapons available by a particular date which would decide the *Wehrmacht*'s 'operational' or 'war-readiness' but rather the availability of raw materials and the capacity of industry to switch over in the shortest possible time to the level of production planned for war. In particular the later head of the War Economy Staff, Major-General Thomas, endeavoured to make use of the chances created by Hitler's fundamental policy decisions to propose comprehensive economic preparation for war.[17] He was initially supported by the Reich Defence Minister, von Blomberg, especially on questions of organisation, but was unable to push through his ideas against the opposition of the three armed services. Despite all the differences which existed on the subject of the armaments economy between those involved, it is nevertheless apparent that the military leadership never questioned the aims of rearmament on economic grounds. Only the means were open to debate. That industry became the instrument for Hitler's political and military goals found the military's unanimous support.

The continuing influence of Hitler's political philosophy on the fundamental political decisions (taken after 1933) in domestic and economic affairs can hardly be denied. Was this also the case in foreign policy? In 1928 Hitler had written that foreign policy was the art of 'securing for a nation the necessary living space in terms of size and wealth'.[18] In February 1933 before the *Reichswehr* generals, he had defined the goals of his foreign policy as the 'struggle against Versailles' and the 'conquest of new living space in the East'. Yet he had also added that the period of the build-up of the *Wehrmacht* would be extremely dangerous and full of risks from the point of view of foreign policy. He said this phase would show whether France really possessed 'statesmen'. If this were the case then it was to be expected that France would regard German rearmament as a reason for 'attacking us (probably with [the help of] their allies in the east)'.[19] To judge from this, it seems that Hitler was aware that the chance of attaining his ultimate ideological goal of 'conquering new living space' depended on specific preconditions. In the phase of the 'rearming' of the nation it was necessary for foreign policy to prevent both the Reich's diplomatic and economic isolation and also any preventive action on the part of the Allies. The Foreign Office, espousing revisionism, fully accepted this diplomatic function in the interest of rearmament.[20] Together with Hitler it was able to achieve significant political successes through various bilateral initiatives, for example the signing of the Concordat on 20 July 1933 and the German–Polish Non-Aggression Pact of 26 January 1934.[21] Hitler himself took every opportunity of emphasising his peaceful intentions and his Propaganda Minister, Dr. Joseph Goebbels, by using large-scale deception was distinctly

successful in his efforts to convince people at home and abroad that
National Socialist policies had peaceful intentions.[22] Each risky but
successful step towards overturning Versailles – October 1933,
March and June 1935 or March 1936 – lessened the threat of a
preventive action by the Allies and increased Hitler's chances of
taking concrete measures towards the realisation of his ultimate
goal. The conference of 5 November 1937 demonstrates in this
connection the continuity and the continuing effectiveness of
Hitler's ideologically-based foreign policy aims.[23]

If one accepts that Hitler was the dominant figure of the National
Socialist régime – and on this there can be no doubt – this justifies
the conclusion that the fundamental decisions of that régime in the
fields of domestic, economic and foreign policy can be summed up
as preparation for war. According to his own ideological convictions, Hitler at no time agreed to an international settlement
which would aim at a lasting peaceful co-existence, at least of the
European nations.[24]

Although, as has already been pointed out, the military leadership showed their broad approval of the régime's notion of domestic
order and the principles of the National Socialist armaments
economy, it is nevertheless still a matter of debate how far this
approval also extended to the long-term goal of Hitler's foreign
policy which could only be realised by a European war. The
evidence suggests that the Social Darwinist basis of Hitler's policy
and the far-reaching consequences involved in the demand for new
living space were either not recognised, were ignored or played
down by the military leadership.[25] The overturning of the Versailles
settlement and the consequent return of the Reich to great power
status had been the central concern of the military elite since 1919.
It was self-evident to the *Reichswehr* leaders that this goal could not
be achieved without the possession of military power, without the
employment of this power and, possibly also, without war. In their
view Hitler's actions in the field of foreign affairs, despite his verbal
excesses and the dubious nature of much of what was happening in
domestic politics, represented a highly successful and vigorous
revisionist policy. The Austrian *Anschluß*, which was carried out
without international complications, was regarded as the culmination of this policy and, broadly speaking, silenced any doubts
which still existed amongst the higher officer corps on the subject of
Hitler's foreign policy.[26] The 'partial identity of aims'[27] between
Hitler and the military leadership in foreign, domestic and

economic affairs lent the régime a large part of its internal stability which in turn reflected the continuity beyond 1933 of the traditional Prussian ideals of political power and internal stability. The positive effect of this climate of general agreement which, as has already been mentioned, did not exclude conflicts on particular points,[28] was considerably reinforced by rearmament, regarded by both sides as the sine qua non for the expansion of the *Wehrmacht*. Rearmament was the indispensable nucleus of German war policy and in this sphere we should no longer speak of a partial identity but rather of a complete identity of aims. Viewed in this light, it becomes clear why Hitler, at least until 1938, left decisions on the scope and the implementation of rearmament almost entirely to the military and only occasionally sought to force the pace even further. In this respect, Army, *Luftwaffe* and Navy armaments planning fulfilled all the régime's expectations. Setbacks and delays in rearmament were in most cases not a result of any lack of determination in the military machine but rather of limited economic resources and the inadequate organisation of the armaments economy.

There was another reason why intervention by Hitler would have been superfluous. After the elimination of the SA in summer 1934, the *Wehrmacht* was the strongest single organisation in the structure of the Third Reich. Although bound by a personal oath to Hitler taken on the death of Hindenburg, the extent of the *Wehrmacht*'s influence within the power structure of the National Socialist régime (which itself has been aptly described as organised chaos[29]) had not yet been decided. But by this time the *Wehrmacht* had already thrown away its chance of extending its share of power. In spite of an initially very favourable position, Blomberg's initiatives had completely failed to produce an integrated *Wehrmacht* command.[30] The political effects of this development secured Hitler's position vis-à-vis the armed forces. The consequences of the expansion of the services in the sphere of armament were more complex. The lack of a comprehensive armaments programme on the one hand prevented any rationalised exploitation of the available but limited economic resources. On the other hand, planning and implementation of the maximal armaments programmes of the three services considerably accelerated the rearmament process. This is clearly seen in the sequence and sum total of the programmes and measures taken by the Army, *Luftwaffe* and Navy in the years 1934–6 and 1938–9. Finally, the three armed services found themselves in a situation of increasing competition with one another in their efforts to rearm which was in general only aggravated by the creation of new institutions with responsibility within the armaments economy. Thus in the armaments sector, a conflict in which the *Wehrmacht* itself played a major role resulted from the jungle of vaguely defined areas of responsibility and the competition for spheres of influence. This state of affairs has been seen as a characteristic feature of the general power structure of the National Socialist régime and one which Hitler favoured. The bureaucratic apparatus of power which had up to that point functioned according to hierarchical principles, became more and more distorted by extreme forms of competition.[31] The powers released by this process reinforced the impression abroad that the seemingly universal political dynamism within Germany went along with an incredibly fast-growing and irresistible military potential.

To return to Hitler's expansionist German policy and its prerequisites, one can see that the balance sheet for the years 1936–8 was extraordinarily favourable. The radical transformation which had taken place in domestic politics as required by the process of 'rearming' Germany was complete and the stability of the régime was not threatened from any quarter. In foreign policy total isolation had been successfully avoided. Hitler had grown convinced that neither France nor Great Britain was either in a position, or willing, to oppose broad revisionist demands by force of arms. Yet there had been no indication that Great Britain was ready to accept the role envisaged for it in the framework of Hitler's *Lebensraum* policy which became prominent from this stage on.[32] Spectacular successes had also been achieved in the build-up of the *Wehrmacht*. Yet in this of all areas the régime came up against barriers which were not to be easily overcome by means of the resources of the National Socialist movement. A state of tension, at first concealed but becoming increasingly more apparent, developed between on the one hand the political goals and the military power necessary to achieve them and on the other economic and, more particularly, armaments resources. This tension was never to be resolved.

The astonishing upward swing taken by the economy after summer 1933 had been prepared by the cabinets of von Papen and Schleicher. But it was the many comprehensive economic measures taken by the Hitler government with the strong support of the

National Socialist movement which produced the real break-through. It has already been indicated that this improvement in the economy was characterised by its armaments components from the beginning.[33] Schacht's financial policies and the reorientation of foreign trade to a great extent served the interests of rearmament. But the economic risks involved in an armaments economy very soon become visible. The shortage of foreign exchange, which had already assumed serious proportions by the end of 1934 and which was in the main caused by the import of raw materials vital to armament, became a feature of the National Socialist armaments economy. Attempts to end the crisis by economic measures in the form of the promotion of exports by the State failed because the economy was confronted not by a reduction but by a further increase in the armed services' armaments orders.[34] The National Socialist leadership reacted to the renewed and extremely unstable situation regarding raw materials with the announcement of the Four Year Plan in September 1936. The plan provided for various measures: the exploitation of all raw materials available within the Reich, ignoring the principle of profitability; the creation and extension of the production of synthetics without reference to the costs involved; it aimed at achieving a high level of self-sufficiency in the space of four years, especially regarding those raw materials necessary for armament and at making the economy as a whole 'ready for war'. This clearly illustrates the Social Darwinist basis of the thoughts and actions of Hitler who could see the sole solution of economic problems in an expansionist war and the acquisition of new living space.

As things stood, Hitler's appeal to the nation in the Four-Year Plan could scarcely bring about any change in the overall economic situation. In winter 1937/8 despite the rationing of raw materials, it became increasingly obvious that the economic means of overcoming the crisis, now aggravated by a manpower shortage, would no longer be sufficient if the existing scope and speed of rearmament were maintained[35] and if the ill effects of the National Socialist power structure, especially evident in the economic sphere, were not overcome. Since both these conditions were of central import-ance to Hitler's policy, a solution to the crisis by these economic means was unlikely from the outset.

The study of the armaments policies of the three armed services has shown that there was no question of going back on their individual armaments intentions for the military leadership as well.

It was only when the situation in the armaments economy left no choice that the process of rearmament was necessarily slowed down. The speed and the almost unrestricted and unco-ordinated armament of the armed services along with political factors led to the complete disregard of the lessons learned from the First World War which had earlier found total acceptance. The comprehensive organisational power of the military, originally regarded as an absolute necessity for a future war, had in the meantime bowed to the control of the armed forces by the Reich's political leadership. One result of this development was that the military very early on gave up the idea of a comprehensive economic preparation for war, that is, 'armament in depth'. Accordingly armaments efforts concentrated on the forces' immediate needs, their primary supply with weapons, equipment and ammunition and limited reserve supplies. Organisational provision was also made for the quickest possible conversion of armaments industries to war production levels, renouncing co-ordination and even disregarding general economic concerns. When from 1936/7 onwards this concept of 'armament in breadth' had reached the limits of economic possibility, the most acceptable solution to the problem seemed to be short predatory wars for the benefit of the armaments economy.[36] The reversal of the relationship of means to ends was almost complete. It was no longer only necessary to rearm in order to wage wars but also necessary to have war in order to continue rearming.

In the face of this development the question arises whether the process of rearmament, which involved and determined large areas of economic and State activity, influenced Hitler's policy and shaped his political decisions. In view of the lack of source material only a vague and tentative answer is possible here. One thing however is not open to doubt: the rearming of the *Wehrmacht* was the sole precondition for the realisation of Hitler's political programme, built as it was around the ideological premises earlier mentioned. There are no known statements which give the slightest ground for believing that Hitler was at any time after 1936 prepared to reduce the scope and speed of armament. The opposite is the case. He attempted to force the process of armament even further although he was aware of the economic and political consequences. There is no doubt that the political reality in Germany prior to the outbreak of the Second World War was characterised to a very great extent by the effects of the military's rearmament measures.[37] The precarious economic situation, the disruption of the State's finances and resulting inflationary tendencies, the State's organisation of manpower potential and concomitant social problems as well as the undeniable *potential* threat posed by the sum of these elements to the domestic power base of the régime cannot, at least from 1936 onwards, be left out of consideration in any assessment of Hitler's war policy. Since Hitler did not even consider an economic solution to the problems, the only other possibility was that of predatory wars as recommended by many economists.[38]

This military and economic situation developed at a time when it was becoming increasingly clear that one of the fundamental assumptions of Hitler's foreign policy proceeded from an incorrect assessment of the interests and reactions of the other European powers. Great Britain showed herself unwilling to accept a German hegemony in Europe based on Hitler's ideals.[39] Yet this political set-back did not cause Hitler to revise his ideologically-based pro-gramme of conquering living space in the east. This was the goal which the build-up of the *Wehrmacht* served and to realise it he was prepared to accept political and military risks. The dimensions of these risks became clear in September 1939. The position at the outbreak of Hitler's war meant that the goal of his own programme was relegated to the distant future. In February 1933 Hitler had described rearmament as the all-important prerequisite for the realisation of his policies. Viewed from the perspective of 1939, armament can be regarded in its political and economic effects as constituting one of the most important driving forces behind German war policy. In other words, although the preconditions for the goal-oriented war policy had *almost* been created, it was the strains imposed by the demands of this policy which ultimately led to its failure.

Notes

NOTES TO FOREWORD

1. 'Until the spring of 1936 "rearmament was largely a myth"', A. J. P. Taylor, 'Second Thoughts', *The Origins of the Second World War* (London: Penguin, 1964) p. 11, citing Burton H. Klein, *Germany's Economic Preparations for War* (Harvard: Harvard University Press, 1959) pp. 16–17.
2. For an important discussion of the relationship between rearmament and the economic policies of the Nazi regime – particularly with reference to employment – see Mason, *Arbeiterklasse und Volksgemeinschaft*, pp. 46–7 and 100 ff. For an indication of the overall cost of German rearmament in peacetime, see Berenice A. Carroll, *Design for Total War. Arms and Economics in the Third Reich* (The Hague, 1968) p. 184, and the very helpful survey of Nazi policies in the fields of armaments, economic planning and diplomacy by William Carr, *Arms, Autarky and Aggression: A Study in German Foreign Policy, 1933–1939* (London, 1972).
3. See below, chapters 4 and 5.
4. See below, p. 90.
5. See below, p. 81.
6. His impatience finds expression in his famous Memorandum on the tasks of the Four-Year Plan in 1936, an English version of which is printed in J. Noakes and G. Pridham, *Documents on Nazism, 1919–1945* (London, 1974) pp. 401–8.
7. This discussion does not, of course, relate only to foreign policy and rearmament, but to the whole decision-making process in the Third Reich, and the character of German National Socialism. A good introduction to the debate is provided by the chapters by K. D. Bracher and H. Mommsen in M. Funke (ed.), *Hitler, Deutschland und die Mächte. Materialien zur Aussenpolitik des Dritten Reiches* (Düsseldorf, 1977).
8. See below, p. 23.
9. See below, p. 39.
10. See below, p. 47–8.
11. See below, p. 49.
12. See note 6.

NOTES TO INTRODUCTION

1. Hans Herzfeld, *Politik, Heer und Rüstung in der Zwischenkriegszeit*, p. 277.
2. Cf. the contribution by several authors entitled 'Zielsetzung und Methode der Militärgeschichtsschreibung', in *Militärgeschichtliche Mitteilungen*, 20 (1976) p. 9 ff.
3. Cf. M. Messerschmidt's summary of existing research, *Militär und Politik in der Bismarckzeit und im Wilhelminischen Deutschland* (Darmstadt, 1975).

4. Cf. V. R. Berghahn (ed.), *Militarismus*, passim; also F. Fischer, Der Stellenwert des Ersten Weltkrieges in der Kontinuitätsproblematik der deutschen Geschichte, in *Historische Zeitschrift*, 229 (1979) pp. 25–53.

5. Note on terminology: According to the Armed Forces Act [*Wehrgesetz*] of 25 March 1921, the *Reichswehr* of the Republic consisted of both the Army (*Reichsheer*) and the Navy (*Reichsmarine*). The *Reichsheer* was subordinate to the Head of the Army Command (*Chef der Heeresleitung*), the *Reichsmarine* to the Head of the Naval Command (*Chef der Marineleitung*). As a result of the legislation on the build-up of the *Wehrmacht* of 16 March 1935 and the Armed Forces Act of 21 May 1935, the *Reichswehr* was replaced by the *Wehrmacht*. At its head stood Colonel-General von Blomberg as Reich Defence Minister (*Reichskriegsminister*) and Commander-in-Chief of the *Wehrmacht* (*Oberbefehlshaber der Wehrmacht*). The *Wehrmacht* comprised the Army (*Heer*) under its Commander-in-Chief (*Oberbefehlshaber des Heeres*) General Freiherr von Fritsch, the Navy (*Kriegsmarine*) under its Commander-in-Chief, Admiral Raeder, and the *Luftwaffe* under the Reich Minister for Aviation and Commander-in-Chief of the *Luftwaffe* (*Reichsminister der Luftfahrt und Oberbefehlshaber der Luftwaffe*) General Hermann Göring.

6. F. L. Carsten, *Reichswehr and Politics*.

7. R. Wohlfeil, *Heer und Republik*.

8. Cf. M. Geyer's summary of literature 'Die Wehrmacht der Republik ist die Reichswehr', in *Militärgeschichtliche Mitteilungen*, 14 (1973) p. 152 ff.; also Müller/Opitz (ed.), *Militär und Militarismus*, passim. The international aspects are discussed comprehensively by E. W. Bennett, *German Rearmament and the West, 1932–1933* (Princeton, 1979).

9. Literally, 'Guilt and Fate': Title of Hermann Foertsch's book on the Fritsch crisis (Stuttgart, 1951).

10. K.-J. Müller, *Das Heer*, passim.

11. Cf. works by M. Messerschmidt, K. H. Völker, E. L. Homze, R. J. Overy, M. Salewski and J. Dülffer.

NOTES TO CHAPTER I

1. Cf. Herzfeld, *Politik, Heer und Rüstung*, p. 264 f.

2. See Wohlfeil, *Heer und Republik*, p. 93 ff.

3. Salewski, *Entwaffnung*, passim.

4. Wohlfeil, *Heer und Republik*, p. 207 f.

5. Stülpnagel papers, BA-MA N 5/10. The *Truppenamt* was, along with other offices, subordinate to the *Chef der Heeresleitung* (see Introduction, Note 5) and took over the functions of the previous General Staff which had been dissolved in accordance with the conditions of the Treaty of Versailles.

6. Geyer, *Aufrüstung*, p. 80 ff.; Carsten, *Reichswehr*, p. 253 ff., interprets this development as a political 'leap to the left'.

7. Carsten, *Reichswehr*, p. 245 ff.; Wohlfeil, *Heer und Republik*, p. 282 ff.

8. Carsten, *Reichswehr*, p. 284 ff.; Wohlfeil, *Heer und Republik*, p. 115 ff.

9. No critical biography of Groener has as yet been written, cf. F. Freiherr Hiller von Gaertringen's contribution in *Neue Deutsche Biographie*, VII (1966), p. 111 ff. for a list of Groener's writings. Cf. also Wohlfeil, *Heer und Republik*, p. 117 ff.; Carsten, *Reichswehr*, p. 290 ff.

10. Cf. the latest account by Gerhard W. Rakenius, *Wilhelm Groener als Erster Generalquartiermeister. Die Politik der Obersten Heersleitung 1918/19* (Boppard 1977), passim and especially the introduction.
11. Cf. Geyer's view in *Aufrüstung*, p. 463 ff.
12. Cf. Wallach's analysis in *Dogma der Vernichtungsschlacht*; also Geyer, *Aufrüstung*, p. 464 ff.
13. Cf. the recently published, B.F. Schulte, 'Neue Dokumente zu Kriegsausbruch und Kriegsverlauf 1914', in *Militärgeschichtliche Mitteilungen*, 25 (1979) pp. 123–85.
14. Memorandum printed in: *Zeitschrift für Geschichtswissenschaft*, xix (1971) pp. 1167 ff.
15. Geyer, *Aufrüstung*, pp. 463 f. and 472 ff.
16. Carsten, *Reichswehr*, p. 265 f.
17. Ibid., pp. 257 ff.
18. Ibid., pp. 220 f. and 266 f.
19. Geyer, *Aufrüstung*, p. 103.
20. Kabinett Müller II/1, No. 42, p. 153.
21. Hansen, *Reichswehr*, pp. 168 ff.; Geyer, *Aufrüstung*, p. 200 f. The A-Army refers to the field army. Cf. Note 32.
22. Cf. Rautenberg, *Rüstungspolitik*, Appendix, p. 81 f. In 1928 the budget of the Reich Army and Ministry amounted to 513.7 thousand million Rm.
23. On the 'Air Force Armament Phase of 1927–31' cf. Hansen, *Reichswehr*, p. 176 ff., and Völker, *Entwicklung*, p. 159 ff.
24. On the activities of the Army Ordnance Office and its Supplies Staff as well as on their objectives cf. Hansen, *Reichswehr*, p. 93 ff.
25. Cf. Geyer, *Rüstungsprogramm*.
26. Groener papers, BA-MA N 46/147. For an interpretation of the memorandum, cf. Dülffer, *Weimar*, p. 113 ff.
27. Cf. Post, *Civil-Military Fabric*, p. 256 ff.
28. Hansen, *Reichswehr*, p. 168 ff. It certainly did not escape Groener's notice that the pocket battleship 'A' was not, according to its construction specifications, suitable for the tasks defined by him in his memorandum 'Das Panzerschiff'. He nevertheless remained of the opinion that the protection of the Baltic and the safeguarding of the link between the Reich and East Prussia was the primary task of the Navy. On the Navy leadership's rejection of this view, see Geyer, *Aufrüstung*, p. 224 ff.; also Schreiber, *Revisionismus*, p. 78 ff. and p. 85 ff.
29. Wohlfeil, *Heer und Republik*, p. 121 ff.; Vogelsang, *Reichswehr*, p. 55 ff.; Carsten, *Reichswehr*, p. 296 ff. The new ministerial department comprised various sections which were directly subordinate to the Minister. As from 30 January 1933 the department was under the direction of Colonel von Reichenau (cf. p. 34 f.) and from 12 February 1934 was designated the *Wehrmachtamt*.
30. Geyer, *Rüstungsprogramm*, p. 131.
31. Directive of 16 April 1930, 147/30, W II a; BA-MA, Pg 34072; Draft in von Bredow papers, BA-MA N 97/9. For an interpretation, see Geyer, *Aufrüstung*, p. 213 ff.; Post, *Civil-Military Fabrics*, p. 197 ff.
32. Cf. Note 25. In German military terminology a basic distinction is drawn between the peacetime army [*Friedensheer*] and the wartime army [*Kriegsheer*] which develops from the peacetime army during the course of mobilisation. The wartime army is composed of the field army [*Feldheer*], i.e. the actual

mobile combat units, and the reserve army [*Ersatzheer*] which remains stationed at home.

33. Post, *Civil-Military Fabric*, p. 204 ff.; Geyer, *Aufrüstung*, p. 188 ff.
34. Geyer, *Aufrüstung*, p. 192 ff.
35. Dülffer, *Weimar*, pp. 67 ff. and 112 ff.; Rahn, *Reichsmarine*, p. 214 ff.
36. On this and the following see Rahn's new account in *Reichsmarine*, p. 114 ff.; also Schreiber, *Reichsmarine*, p. 162 ff. Dülffer, *Determinanten*, p. 15 f. speaks of a crisis of status in the Navy between 1928 and 1932.
37. Geyer, *Aufrüstung*, p. 195 ff., especially Note 27. On the Navy's studies, see also Rahn, *Reichsmarine*, p. 133 ff.; Schreiber, *Revisionismus*, p. 51 ff.; Schreiber, *Reichsmarine*, p. 160 ff.
38. Cf. Note 26.
39. Cf. Note 28.
40. Geyer, *Aufrüstung*, pp. 197 ff. and 207 ff.; Post, *Civil-Military Fabric*, p. 215 ff.
41. Geyer, *Aufrüstung*, p. 207 f.; Post, *Civil-Military Fabric*, p. 152 ff.
42. Geyer, *Aufrüstung*, p. 208 ff.; Post, *Civil-Military Fabric*, p. 162 ff.
43. Cf. Geyer, *Landesverteidigung*, p. 166 ff.
44. Vogelsang, *Reichswehr*, p. 132 f.
45. Cf. Groener-Geyer, *Groener*, p. 270 ff.; Carsten, *Reichswehr*, p. 321 f.
46. On the entire issue see Bucher, *Reichswehrprozeß*, p. 122 ff. and 143 ff.; Carsten, *Reichswehr*, p. 347 ff.
47. According to article 1 of the 'Professional Duties of the Soldier' in the edition of 5 September 1930, the soldier was duty-bound to show loyalty to the republican constitution cf. Absolon, *Wehrmacht*, vol. 1, p. 172 f.
48. Cf. Meier-Welcker, *Briefwechsel*, p. 71 ff.
49. Ibid., especially Note 57.
50. Wohlfeil, *Heer und Republik*, p. 289 ff.; Carsten, *Reichswehr*, p. 309 ff.; Vogelsang, *Reichswehr* p. 113 ff.
51. Vogelsang, *Reichswehr*, p. 135 ff.
52. Reich President von Hindenburg had been re-elected on 23 March and 10 April 1932. Elections to the *Länder* parliaments took place on 24 April 1932 in Prussia, Bavaria, Württemberg, Hamburg and Anhalt.
53. Vogelsang, *Reichswehr*, p. 166 ff.
54. Vogelsang, *Reichswehr*, p. 170 ff.; cf. also Geyer, *Aufrüstung*, p. 270 f.; Sauer *Mobilmachung*, p. 35 ff. On Schleicher's policy while Reich Defence Minister under Papen, and from 2 December 1932 as Reich Chancellor cf. Vogelsang, *Schleicher*, p. 75 ff.; Carsten, *Reichswehr*, p. 327 ff. Schleicher's policy at the Geneva Disarmament Conference met with some success: on 11 December 1932 military parity for Germany was acknowledged in principle in a five-power agreement. In domestic politics, however, his attempts to 'tame' Hitler and the National Socialist movement, and with the aid of the *Reichswehr* to create a power base which was fundamentally extra-parliamentary, failed. Cf. also below p. 25.

NOTES TO CHAPTER 2

1. Cf. Wollstein, *Revisionismus*, p. 23 ff.; Carsten, *Reichswehr*, p. 393 f.; Vogelsang, *Reichswehr*, p. 397 ff.
2. For Hitler's speech of 3 February 1933 which must be seen in conjunction with

Blomberg's statement to the cabinet of 30 January 1933 see Vogelsang, *Dokumente*, p. 434 f.

3. On this episode see especially Wollstein, *Revisionismus*, p. 45 ff.
4. *Akten zur deutschen auswärtigen Politik (ADAP)*, C, I/1, No. 26, p. 55 f.
5. *ADAP*, C, I/1, No. 94, p. 173 f.
6. *ADAP*, C, I/1, No. 106, p. 190.
7. Cf. Wollstein, *Revisionismus*, p. 96 ff.
8. On the German attitude to the Macdonald Plan and the Four Power Pact, cf. especially Wollstein, *Revisionismus*, p. 64 ff. and p. 147 ff.
9. Wollstein, *Revisionismus*, p. 190 ff.
10. Wollstein, *Revisionismus*, p. 187; Quotation *ADAP*, C, I/2, No. 475, p. 868.
11. Cf. above, p. 12 ff.
12. Cf. especially, Vogelsang, *Reichswehr*, pp. 225 ff. and 294 ff.
13. Cf. above, p. 16 f.
14. Cf. Carsten, *Reichswehr*, p. 389 ff.; Vogelsang, *Reichswehr*, p. 397 ff.
15. Cf. Vogelsang, *Reichswehr*, p. 285 ff.; Rautenberg, *Rüstungspolitik*, p. 239 ff.; Geyer, *Aufrüstung*, p. 295 ff.
16. Carsten, *Reichswehr*, p. 387 f.; Geyer, *Aufrüstung*, pp. 290 f., 303 f. and 307 f.
17. Geyer, *Aufrüstung*, p. 307 ff.
18. Cf. Note 2.
19. Quoted by Müller, *Heer*, p. 63.
20. Cf. Sauer, *Mobilmachung*, p. 234 ff.; Bennecke, *SA*, p. 212 ff., who also includes data on the strength of the *SA* from 1933 to 1935; further figures are to be found in Sauer, *Mobilmachung*, pp. 223 and 268, as well as in Kater, *Soziologie der SA*, p. 799. On *Stahlhelm* see V. R. Berghahn, *Der Stahlhelm. Bund der Frontsoldaten 1918–1935* (Düsseldorf, 1966).
21. Here cf. especially, Sauer, *Mobilmachung*, p. 255 ff.; Müller, *Heer*, p. 88 ff.
22. Summed up in Wollstein, *Revisionismus*, p. 203 ff., espec. p. 206.
23. Sauer, *Mobilmachung*, p. 266 ff.; Rautenberg, *Rüstungspolitik*, p. 241 ff.; Rautenberg, *Dokumente*, p. 108 f.
24. Absolon, *Wehrmacht*, vol. 2, p. 487; *IMT*, vol. 29, p. 4. A comparison of figures alone between the 100,000-man regular army and the 250,000-man force demanded by Hitler from the militia, which the SA and its leader Röhm intended to form, reveals how precarious the situation was in which the *Reichswehr* leadership increasingly found itself. Röhm's military intentions were well known. In early 1933 he had described himself to Rauschning as the 'Scharnhorst of the new army'; that his aim was the creation of a new SA People's Army which would incorporate the *Reichswehr*, although not, of course, its generals. Cf. here Sauer, *Mobilmachung*, p. 255 ff.
25. Cf. Meier-Welcker, *Briefwechsel*, p. 89 ff.; Rautenberg, *Dokumente*, p. 119, espec. Note 118 f.
26. Rautenberg in *Rüstungspolitik*, p. 224 f., has endeavoured to compile figures on the demands made on the *Reichswehr* by the training measures for early summer 1933. According to these, 60 per cent of the younger officers were involved, this figure not including SA camps. On the loss of personnel to the emergent *Luftwaffe* see Rautenberg, *Dokumente*, p. 125, espec. Note 213.
27. Absolon, *Wehrmacht*, vol. 2, p. 493 ff. (6 November and 1 December 1933).
28. Cf. Geyer, *Rüstungsprogramm*, passim. cf. also Chap. 1, Note 32.

29. Cf. Rautenberg, *Rüstungspolitik*, p. 216 ff.; Rautenberg, *Dokumente*, p. 103 ff.; Dülffer, *Weimar*, p. 231 ff., and also file BA-MA 15/v. 287.

30. Cf. Vogelsang, *Dokumente*, p. 434.

31. Geyer, *Rüstungsprogramm*, p. 134 ff.; Dülffer, *Weimar*, p. 239 ff.

32. Rautenberg, *Rüstungspolitik*, pp. 217 ff., 220 ff. and 235 ff.; Rautenberg, *Dokumente*, p. 107 f., and especially Note 142.

33. Wollstein, *Revisionsismus*, pp. 229 ff. and 238 ff.

34. On the *Reichswehr* leadership's planning decisions of December 1933 see Geyer, *Aufrüstung*, p. 329 ff.; also Rautenberg's comprehensive contribution in *Dokumente*, p. 110 ff.; cf. also Müller, *Beck-Studien*, Doc. No. 9 (Memorandum of 14 December 1933); Cf. also Chap. 1, Note 32.

35. Cf. Rautenberg, *Dokumente*, p. 119. Cf. also Note 24 above. At a Commanders' conference of 2 February 1934, Blomberg stated that Röhm had declared in a memorandum that 'the entire sphere of national defence' was the 'domain of the SA'. Thus up to this point of time, all attempts by the *Reichswehr* leadership, and especially Reichenau, to gain a decisive influence on the military training of the enormous number of potential recruits in the SA (circa one million active SA members between the ages of 18 and 35) had failed. After Hitler at a conference on 28 February 1934 came down in favour of the *Reichswehr*, the course was set for the conflict which Hitler brought to a close with the purge of 30 June 1934. Cf. especially Sauer, *Mobilmachung*, p. 324 ff.

36. Talk by the head of the Army Ordnance Office of 9 May 1934 (H.Wa.A. No. 875/34 g.Kdos WiI, BA-MA Wi/I F 5/1638); the quotations are taken from this talk.

37. Commanders' conference of 3 February 1933, cf. Vogelsang, *Dokumente*, p. 433.

38. Liebmann's notes on the Commanders' conference of 1 March 1933 Institut für Zeitgeschichte, Archiv, ED 1, vol. 1.

39. On Blomberg's attitude to Hitler and the NS movement cf. Müller, *Heer*, pp. 49 ff. and 61 ff.

40. Taken from Messerschmidt, *Wehrmacht*, p. 488.

41. Müller, *Heer*, p. 47.

42. Müller, *Heer*, p. 71 ff.

43. Müller, *Heer*, pp. 68 and 78.

44. On the Röhm Affair see especially Müller, *Heer*, pp. 95 ff. and 125 ff.; on the form and extent of co-operation with the political squads of the SS and Himmler's SD see, Müller, *Röhm-Affäre*, p. 107 ff.; Cf. also Sauer, *Mobilmachung*, p. 324 ff.

45. Cf. Müller, *Heer*, p. 134 ff.

46. Blomberg, speaking at the Commanders' conference of 12 January 1935, taken from, Müller, *Heer*, p. 167.

47. Cf. Müller, *Heer*, p. 147 f.; also Höhne, *Orden*, p. 407 f.

48. On the lack of co-operation between the services in the field of armaments cf. below, p. 91 ff.

49. Cf. Messerschmidt, *Wehrmacht*, p. 210, Note 746, cf. also Kotze, *Heeresadjudant*, p. 20.

NOTES TO CHAPTER 3

1. Rautenberg, *Dokumente*, p. 119 ff.
2. Cf. here Wollstein, *Revisionismus*, p. 249 ff. and also Hildebrand, *Foreign Policy*, p. 24 ff.
3. On Hitler's demands see Geyer, *Militär*, p. 260 but also see Müller, *Heer*, p. 208. On the size of the army, as mentioned below, see Rautenberg, *Rüstungspolitik*, p. 312.
4. Cf. above p. 16 f.
5. Cf. Rautenberg, *Dokumente*, pp. 107 and 120 f.
6. Ibid., p. 121.
7. Absolon, *Wehrmacht*, vol. 3, p. 6 ff.; Müller, *Heer*, p. 208 f.; Hoßbach, *Wehrmacht*, p. 81 ff.; Foerster, *Beck*, p. 34.
8. Cf. Müller's exposition in *Heer*, p. 208 f.
9. The memorandum is printed in Müller, *Beck-Studien*, Doc. No. 24. Comment of Colonel-General von Fritsch of 11 March 1935, BA-MA, RH 2/v. 1022; cf. also Chap. 1, Note 32.
10. On the factual organisational development of the army build-up cf. Schottelius/Caspar, *Organisation des Heeres*, p. 295 ff.
11. Cf. Geyer, Aufrüstung, p. 212 f.
12. Cf. Geyer, *Militär*, p. 253.
13. Memorandum of 14 February 1936 from the 5th Div. of the General Staff, BA-MA, II H593/3.
14. Cf. Hansen, *Reichswehr*, pp. 68 f. and 138 ff.
15. J. T. Emmerson, *The Rhineland Crisis*, passim, and especially M. Funke, '7 März 1936. Fallstudie zum aussenpolitischen Führungsstil Hitlers', W. Michalka (ed.), *Nationalsozialistische Aussenpolitik* (Darmstadt, 1978) pp. 277–324.
16. T.A. No. 1800/35 g.Kdos of 24 June 1935; BA-MA RH 2/v. 1019.
17. Cf. his comment of 15 June 1935 PA No. 450/35 g.Kdos; BA-MA RH 2/v. 1019.
18. Cf. Rautenberg, *Dokumente*, p. 122.
19. Cf. Absolon, *Wehrmacht*, vol. 3, p. 162, in connection with the strength of the Reich Army of circa 400,000 men reached by autumn 1935.
    The E-Officer Corps ('E' stands for 'supplementary') was made up of former officers who had either served the *Reichswehr* already as civilian employees during the Republic or who now saw in rearmament the opportunity to return to their former careers.
20. See Model, *Generalstabsoffizier*, p. 21 ff. (1st and 2nd Parts); also J. Fischer's review of the book in *Militärgeschichtliche Mitteilungen*, 5 (1969) p. 199 ff.
21. Cf. his comment of 9 July 1935; BA-MA RH 2/v. 1019.
22. Cf. also Geyer, *Militär*, p. 261 f.; also Schottelius/Caspar, *Organisation des Heeres*, pp. 297, 302 f. and 351 f.
23. Cf. R. Barthel, *Theorie und Praxis der Heeresmotorisierung*.
24. Literature on Guderian and on the development of the German tank force is listed in the two newest biographies of the General: Macksey, *Guderian* and Walde, *Guderian*. Cf. also W. Deist, *De Gaulle et Guderian*, p. 47 ff.
25. Guderian, *Erinnerungen*, pp. 23 f. and 29 f.; Nehring, *Geschichte der deutschen Panzerwaffe*, p. 88 f.

26. Cf. the comment of the Army Ordnance Office (Bb. No. 431/35 g.Kdos) of 30 October 1935; BA-MA ii H 630.
27. The document is now printed in Müller, *Beck-Studien*, Doc. Nos. 31 and 39.
28. Here cf. also H. Senff, *Die Entwicklung der Panzerwaffe.*
29. Cf. his comment of 30 January 1936, printed in Müller, *Beck-Studien*, Doc. No. 39.
30. Comment of 9 January 1936 (O. Q. I/2. Abt. No. 15/36 g.Kdos); BA-MA ii H 622.
31. Cf. above p. 31.
32. Cf. Schottelius/Caspar, *Organisation des Heeres*, p. 303 f.
33. Generalstab des Heeres O.Q. 1/2. Abt. No. 500/36 g.Kdos of 1 April 1936; BA-MA H 1/120; cf. also Schottelius/Caspar, *Organisation des Heeres*, p. 304.
34. Generalstab des Heeres, 2 Abt.Nr. 929/36 g.Kdos of 12 June 1936; BA-MA RH 2/v. 1021. This document gives the date of the conference on 8 June 1936.
35. Correspondence No. 983/36 g.Kdos; BA-MA RH 2/v. 1015.
36. On the strength of the Officer Corps on 6 October 1936 cf. Absolon, *Wehrmacht*, vol. 3, p. 162.
37. See note 34.
38. On Beck's views on foreign policy see Müller's penetrating analysis in, *Beck-Studien*, Chap. 4.
39. AHA No. 1790/36 g.Kdos of 1 August 1936; BA-MA RH 15/70.
40. According to Fromm's data, unspecified 'Wechselunkosten' were to be added to the new financial requirement for which previously an annual total of 700 million Rm. had to be found.
41. Cf. here appendix 11 to the submission by the General Army Office of 1 August 1936. Cf. also Geyer, *Militär*, p. 264 ff.
42. Institut für Zeitgeschichte, Archiv, ED, vol. 1. Liebmann's notes on a meeting of the Commanders on 2 February 1934.
43. AHA No. 2300/36 g.Kdos of 12 October 1936; BA-MA RH 15/70.
44. Cf. here G. Thomas, *Wehr- und Rüstungswirtschaft*, p. 62 ff. On the function of the Army Economic Staff cf. Volkmann, *NS-Wirtschaft*, p. 229 ff.
45. File note of 7 December 1936, 'aus der Besprechung beim Herrn Ob.d.H. am Samstag, dem 6.xii.36'; BA-MA RH 15/70.
46. Cf. here the contributions of W. A. Boelcke, D. Petzina, T. W. Mason and A. S. Milward in Forstmeier and Volkmann, *Wirtschaft und Rüstung.*
47. Cf. D. Petzina, 'Vierjahresplan und Rüstungspolitik', p. 65 ff. in the volume mentioned in note 46.
48. M. Domarus, *Hitler, Reden und Proklamationen, 1932–1945*, vol. 1, p. 637.
49. Cf. Petzina, *Autarkiepolitik*, p. 40 ff.
50. Letter from Blomberg to Göring of 31 August 1936; IMT, vol. 37, p. 153 f.
51. Note from Colonel Thomas of 2 September 1936; IMT, vol. 37, p. 153 f. Cf. also W. Treue, 'Hitlers Denkschrift zum Vierjahresplan 1936', in *Vierteljahrshefte für Zeitgeschichte*, 3 (1955), p. 184 ff.
52. On the strength of the *Luftwaffe* at the outbreak of war cf. p. 58 and p. 90; on the strength of the Navy at the same juncture cf. p. 81 f.

1. Cf. Völker, *Entwicklung der militärischen Luftfahrt*, p. 125 ff.; Rautenberg, *Rüstungspolitik*, p. 317 ff.; Homze, *Arming*, p. 1 ff.; Völker, *Luftwaffe 1933–39*, p. 28 f.; Irving, *Luftwaffe*, p. 54 ff.
2. Völker, *Entwicklung der militärischen Luftfahrt*, p. 201 ff.; Völker, *Dokumente*, No. 41, p. 131 ff.; Irving, *Luftwaffe*, p. 64 f.
3. Cf. Heimann/Schunke, *Denkschrift*, p. 72 ff. On Knauss also cf. Rautenberg/Wiggershaus, 'Die Himmeroder Denkschrift vom Oktober 1950', in *Militärgeschichtliche Mitteilungen*, 21 (1977), pp. 150 ff. and 189. According to this Knauss played a decisive part not only in the conception of the *Luftwaffe* in the Third Reich but also in that of the Federal German Air Force.
4. This particular term does not appear in the memorandum.
5. On the discussion of 3 February 1933 cf. above p. 26. On the assessment of the threat to armament policy posed by the military cf. the memorandum of March 1933 from the Chief of the *Truppenamt*, General Adam, (Sta Nürnberg, X VDB (d) Krupp No. 26, pp. 25–32) and also Beck's memorandum of 20 May 1934 (Müller, *Beck-Studien*, Doc. No. 11 and the interpretation ibid., Chap. 4).
6. Cf. below p. 71 f.
7. Irving, *Luftwaffe*, p. 32 ff.; Homze, *Arming*, p. 74 f.; Völker, *Entwicklung der militärischen Luftfahrt*, p. 212 f.; Rautenberg, *Rüstungspolitik*, Appendix p. 89 f.
8. Irving, *Luftwaffe*, p. 38 f.
9. M. Howard, *The Continental Commitment: The dilemma of British defence policy in the era of the two world wars* (London, 1972) p. 108 ff.
10. On these negotiations cf. Wollstein, *Revisionismus*, p. 249 ff.
11. Institut für Zeitgeschichte, Archiv, ED 1, vol. 1 (Liebmann's notes on the Commanders' conference of 1 June 1933).
12. Ibid. Notes on the conferences of 3 October 1933 and 2 February and 27 February 1934.
13. Völker, *Luftwaffe 1933–39*, pp. 56, 125 and 183.
14. Ibid. pp. 52 ff. and 121 ff.; Boog, *Offizierkorps der Luftwaffe*, p. 269 ff.
15. Völker, *Dokumente*, No. 80, p. 194 f.
16. Ibid., No. 82, p. 197 f.
17. Völker, *Luftwaffe 1933–39*, p. 57; Rautenberg, *Rüstungspolitik*, App. p. 91.
18. Völker, *Luftwaffe 1933–39*, p. 24; Irving, *Luftwaffe*, p. 34 f.; Homze, *Arming*, p. 73.
19. Irving, *Luftwaffe*, p. 32 f.
20. On the figures cf. Homze, *Arming*, pp. 78 f., 93 and 184 ff.
21. Ibid., p. 62 ff., p. 77 ff.; Irving, *Luftwaffe*, pp. 34 f., 76 and 403 (Note 92).
22. Völker, *Dokumente*, No. 82, p. 197 f.
23. On the Wehrmacht Study 1933/4 from the Luftwaffe's point of view cf. Völker, *Dokumente*, No. 184, p. 429 f.; Rautenberg, *Rüstungspolitik*, p. 325.
24. Völker, *Luftwaffe 1933–39*, p. 56 f.; Rautenberg, *Rüstungspolitik*, p. 325 f., App. p. 91; Homze, *Arming*, p. 79 ff.; Overy, *Production Plans*, p. 779 f.
25. Irving, *Luftwaffe*, p. 42 f.
26. Overy, *Production Plans*, p. 780.
27. Völker, *Dokumente*, No. 182, p. 428 f.; Rautenberg, *Rüstungspolitik*, p. 321 ff., App. p. 89 f. On the use of the term 'operational Luftwaffe' cf. Köhler, *Operativer Luftkrieg*, p. 265 ff.

28. Homze, *Arming*, p. 93; Völker, *Luftwaffe 1933–39*, p. 57.
29. Cf. Note 22.
30. Cf. Völker, *Luftwaffe 1933–39*, p. 58 f.; Homze, *Arming*, p. 82 ff., espec. p. 84.
31. Cf. Homze, *Arming*, p. 103 ff. For a survey of the quick succession of programmes see Overy, *Production Plans*, p. 780 ff.; on the conversion phase of 1937 cf. Völker, *Luftwaffe 1933–39*, p. 131 ff.; Murray, *German Air Power*, p. 110.
32. Homze, *Arming*, p. 120 f.
33. Irving, *Luftwaffe*, p. 54; Homze, *Arming*, p. 121 ff.; Völker, *Luftwaffe 1933–39*, p. 132 f.; nevertheless this did not mean that the demand for a four-engined bomber for the German *Luftwaffe* was completely struck from the list of intended developments. Proof of this can be seen in the changing fortunes of the He 177 (Kens-Nowarra, *Flugzeuge*, p. 292 ff.).
34. Völker, *Dokumente*, No. 200, p. 466 ff. On the Luftwaffe's concept of air warfare cf. especially Maier, *Aufbau der Luftwaffe*, ms., passim.
35. Cf. Maier, *Guernica*, passim.
36. On the question of organisational changes v. espec. Völker, *Luftwaffe 1933–39*, pp. 75 ff. and 166 ff. For decisions on personnel Irving, *Luftwaffe*, pp. 50 ff.; Homze, *Arming*, p. 233 f.
37. Ibid., p. 156 f.; Völker, *Luftwaffe 1933–39*, p. 132 ff.
38. Cf. Udet's speech at the Commanders' conference on 6 October 1936, BA-MA RL 3/55.
39. Cf. Homze, *Arming*, p. 163 ff.; Irving, *Luftwaffe*, p. 64 f.; Völker, *Luftwaffe 1933–39*, p. 190.
40. Irving, *Luftwaffe*, p. 95 f.
41. Ibid., p. 64 f.; Homze, *Arming*, pp. 156 f. and 163 f.; Kens-Nowarra, *Flugzeuge*, p. 365.
42. Overy, *Production Plans*, p. 781; Homze, *Arming*, pp. 102 ff., 149 ff., 159 and 222 ff. According to Homze, *Arming*, p. 159, *two* different sources give the following figures for actual aircraft production for 1934–9: 1934: 1968/1817; 1935: 3183/3307; 1936: 5112/5248; 1937: 5606/5749; 1938: 5235/5316; 1939: 8295/7582; aircraft of all types.
43. Völker, *Dokumente*, No. 196, p. 449 f.; for an interpretation see espec. Maier, *Aufbau der Luftwaffe*, ms., p. 10 ff.
44. Cf. Völker, *Dokumente*, No. 46, p. 137 ff.; No. 173, p. 413 ff.; No. 176, p. 420. Völker, *Luftwaffe 1933–39*, p. 105 f.; Irving, *Luftwaffe*, p. 91.
45. Cf. Gundelach, *Gedanken*, p. 33; Gemzell, *Raeder*, p. 178 ff.
46. BA-MA, PG/33272, Case GE 1165 (RML u. ObdL Genstb. 1. Abt. Nr. 144/38 g.Kdos. vom 20.5.38).
47. Gundelach, *Gedanken*, p. 35 ff.; Völker, *Dokumente*, No. 199, p. 460.; Maier, *Aufbau der Luftwaffe*, ms., p. 14 ff.
48. Cf. IMT, vol. 32, p. 334 ff. (Conference of 2 December 1936), as well as *IMT*, vol. 27, p. 160 ff. (Conference of 14 October 1938).

NOTES TO CHAPTER 5

1. Salewski, *Marineleitung*, pp. 126 and 154.
2. For details on regulations governing the Navy cf. Güth, *Organisation der Marine 1913–1933*, p. 322 ff.; Dülffer, *Reichs- und Kriegsmarine*, p. 353 ff.
3. Dülffer, *Weimar*, p. 232; on the size of the fleet cf. the data on construction

given by J. Rohwer in Dülffer, *Weimar*, p. 570 ff.

4. On this see especially Rahn, *Reichsmarine*, p. 117 ff.; Post, *Civil-Military Fabric*, p. 239 ff.; Dülffer, *Weimar*, p. 192 ff.; Schreiber, *Revisionismus*, p. 39 ff.

5. Cf. above p. 28 f.

6. For details on the conversion plan cf. Güth, *Organisation der Kriegsmarine*, pp. 405 ff.; Dülffer, *Reichs- und Kriegsmarine*, p. 437 ff.; on internal criticism within the Navy cf. Dülffer, *Weimar*, p. 233.

7. Salewski, *Marineleitung*, p. 121 ff.; Dülffer, *Weimar*, pp. 204 ff.

8. Cf. here Knauss' comments above, p. 56.

9. Salewski, *Marineleitung*, pp. 125 ff. and 153 ff. (facsimile edition); Dülffer, *Weimar*, p. 244 ff.

10. Dülffer's argument (ibid., p. 245) attributing this comment to Hitler is not convincing from the point of view of form and content; cf. Salewski, *Marineleitung*, p. 126.

11. Dülffer, *Weimar*, p. 248 f.

12. Ibid., p. 249; Raeder's choice of words is revealing.

13. Dülffer, *Weimar*, p. 566; Dülffer, *Reichs- und Kriegsmarine*, p. 464.; Güth, *Organisation der Kriegsmarine*, pp. 414 f. On 1 April 1934 the fleet consisted of the following ships, all built since the First World War. 1 pocket battleship (the 'Deutschland'), 5 light cruisers (the *Emden, Königsberg, Karlsruhe, Köln* and *Leipzig*), 12 torpedo boats, 8 minesweepers and 8 small torpedo boats. Training and support vessels are not included in the figures.

14. Dülffer, *Weimar*, p. 251 ff.; Salewski, *Marineleitung*, p. 138 f.

15. Salewski, *Seekriegsleitung I*, p. 8.

16. Cf. here Schreiber, *Revisionismus*, p. 54 f.

17. Dülffer, *Weimar*, p. 275.

18. Salewski, *Seekriegsleitung I*, p. 13; Dülffer, *Reichs- und Kriegsmarine*, p. 454 f.

19. On the international naval agreement after the First World War, cf. Dülffer, *Weimar*, p. 130 ff. The Washington Agreement had laid down the relative sizes of the fleets of the USA, Great Britain, Japan, France and Italy at 5:5:5:1.75:1.75.

20. Dülffer, *Weimar*, p. 283 ff.; Salewski, *Seekriegsleitung I*, p. 13 f.; Salewski, *Marineleitung*, p. 138 f.

21. Salewski, *Marineleitung*, p. 136 f.

22. Dülffer, *Weimar*, p. 286 ff.; Salewski, *Seekriegsleitung I*, p. 14 f.; Salewski, *Marineleitung*, p. 138 ff.

23. Salewski, *Marineleitung*, pp. 140 ff. and 156 f.; Dülffer, *Weimar*, p. 288 ff.; Dülffer, *Reichs-und Kriegsmarine*, p. 455. Both authors assume that it was Hitler, not Raeder, who mentioned the idea that the fleet might later be used against Britain. The *Scharnhorst* and *Gneisenau* were henceforth to be constructed as battleships, each with a size of 31,800 tons and nine 28 cm guns.

24. For a summary of the discussions cf. Dülffer, *Reichs- und Kriegsmarine*, pp. 454 ff. and 524 (bibliography).

25. Cf. especially Salewski, *Marineleitung*, p. 146 f.; Dülffer, *Weimar*, p. 312 ff.; the development of data on the later *Bismarck* is very revealing.

26. Salewski, *Marineleitung*, p. 148.

27. Ibid., p. 149.

28. Schreiber, *Revisionismus*, p. 102. Since June 1935 the Navy had been termed the 'War Navy' (*Kriegsmarine*). From this point on, Raeder's title was

Commander-in-Chief of the *Kriegsmarine*, cf. Güth, *Organisation der Kriegsmarine*, p. 420.

29. Dülffer, *Weimar*, p. 435 f.; Salewski, *Seekriegsleitung I*, p. 32 f.; Schreiber, *Revisionismus*, p. 105.

30. Dülffer, *Reichs- und Kriegsmarine*, p. 470 ff.; Schreiber, *Revisionismus*, p. 100 ff.

31. Salewski, *Seekriegsleitung I*, p. 20 ff., especially p. 30 ff.; Schreiber, *Revisionismus*, p. 102 f., p. 110. On the demands for bases cf. especially Gemzell, *Raeder*, pp. 45 ff., 58 ff., 97 ff. and 113 ff.; Gemzell, *Organisation*, p. 278 ff.

32. On the conference of 5 November 1937 cf. Müller, *Heer*, p. 243 ff.; Dülffer, *Weimar*, p. 447 ff.; Reynolds, *Treason*, p. 102 f.; Carr, *Rüstung*, p. 438 ff.; also Messerschmidt, *Aussenpolitik*, pp. 423 ff., and the recent literature mentioned therein. Cf. also Chap. 6, Note 38. On the May Crisis of 1938 cf. Note 36 below.

33. Dülffer, *Weimar*, p. 446 ff.; Dülffer, *Reichs- und Kriegsmarine*, p. 477 f.

34. Cf. Salewski, *Selbstverständnis*, p. 69 ff.; Salewski in *England*, p. 177 over-emphasises the influence Hitler's British policy had on naval armaments policy.

35. At the conference on the conclusion of the 1937/38 manoeuvres in Kiel on 12 April 1938, cf. Dülffer, *Weimar*, p. 461 ff.

36. Salewski, *Seekriegsleitung I*, p. 41 ff.; Dülffer, *Weimar*, p. 468 ff.; Gemzell, *Raeder*, p. 79 ff.; Dülffer, *Reichs- und Kriegsmarine*, p. 479f.

37. Salewski, *Seekriegsleitung I*, p. 44 ff.; Dülffer, *Weimar*, p. 475 ff.; Dülffer, *Reichs- und Kriegsmarine*, p. 480 ff. The final version of the memorandum of 25 October 1938 is to be found in Salewski, *Seekriegsleitung III*, p. 28 ff.

38. Salewski, *Seekriegsleitung I*, p. 55 f.; Dülffer, *Weimar*, p. 486 ff.; Gemzell, *Raeder*, p. 87 ff. On a further memorandum of Carls cf. Gemzell, *Raeder*, p. 97 ff.

39. Güth, *Organisation der Kriegsmarine*, pp. 415 ff. and 431 ff., espec. p. 443; *IMT*, vol. 35, p. 571.

40. Dülffer, *Weimar*, p. 563.

41. Cf. the construction data given by J. Rohwer in Dülffer, *Weimar*, p. 570 ff.

42. Quoted from Dülffer, *Weimar*, p. 315.

43. Cf. here Dülffer, *Reichs- und Kriegsmarine*, p. 473 ff.

44. On shipbuilding delays cf. Dülffer, *Weimar*, p. 568 f.

45. On the construction plan of 21 December 1937 cf. Dülffer, *Weimar*, p. 455.

46. Salewski, *Seekriegsleitung I*, p. 37 f.; Dülffer, *Weimar*, p. 452 ff., espec. p. 458 ff.

47. On the so-called 'Z-Plan Fleet', the development of individual variations within the plan and on its implementation in 1939, cf: Salewski, *Seekriegsleitung I*, p. 57 f.; Salewski, *Seekriegsleitung III*, p. 62 f.; Dülffer, *Weimar*, p. 492 ff.; Dülffer, *Reichs- und Kriegsmarine*, p. 482 ff.; Güth, *Organisation der Kriegsmarine*, p. 451 f.

48. Dülffer, *Weimar*, p. 496 f.

49. Cf. ibid., p. 497 f., espec. p. 502.

50. Quoted from Wagner, *Lagevorträge*, p. 20 f.

51. On the studies cf. Dülffer, *Weimar*, p. 526 ff.

52. Cf. W. Deist, 'Die Politik der Seekriegsleitung und die Rebellion der Flotte Ende Oktober 1918', in *Vierteljahrshefte für Zeitgeschichte*, 14 (1966) pp. 341–68.

NOTES TO CHAPTER 6

1. Cf. K. Maier, H. Rohde, B. Stegemann and H. Umbreit, 'Die Errichtung der Hegemonie über Europa 1939–1941,' *Das Deutsche Reich und der Zweite Weltkrieg*, 2 (Stuttgart, 1979).
2. Cf. above pp. 50 ff., 66 ff., 84 f.
3. Chef des Heereswaffenamtes, Nr. 1392/36 g.kdos vom 10 November 1936; BA-MA RH 2/v. 240.
4. Oberbefehlshaber des Heeres, Nr. 64/39 g.kdos vom 10 February 1939; BA-MA III H 98/4.
5. AHA Nr. 567/37 g.kdos vom 11 March 1937; BA-MA III H 98/1.
6. Oberkommando des Heeres, Nr. 2798/37 g.kdos vom 14 December 1937; BA-MA III H 98/2.
7. Cf. Volkmann, *NS-Wirtschaft*, p. 359 ff.
8. AHA Nr. 1220/39 g.kdos 15 April 1939; BA-MA III H 98/5.
9. Cf. Domarus, *Hitler Reden, II*, p. 1156.
10. Cf. Hummelberger, *Rüstungsindustrie*, in Forstmeier and Volkmann, *Wirtschaft und Rüstung*, p. 308 ff., espec. Note 13.
11. Schottelius/Caspar, *Organisation des Heeres*, pp. 315, 318 and 386 ff.; Mueller-Hillebrand, *Heer, I*, p. 65 ff.
12. Cf. above p. 66 f.
13. Völker, *Dokumente*, No. 89, p. 211 f.; Homze, *Arming*, p. 222 ff.; Overy, *Production Plans*, pp. 782 f. and 787 ff.; Irving, *Luftwaffe*, p. 67 f.
14. Irving, *Luftwaffe*, p. 67; Völker, *Luftwaffe 1933–39*, p. 138; Homze, *Arming*, p. 223; Volkmann, *NS-Wirtschaft*, pp. 304 f. and 359 f.
15. Cf. Murray, *German Air Power*, p. 107 ff.
16. Völker, *Luftwaffe 1933–39*, p. 174 f.; Köhler Hummel, *Organisation der Luftwaffe*, p. 570 f.
17. Cf. above p. 68 f.
18. Cf. above p. 84.
19. Cf. above p. 82 ff.
20. Cf. Meier-Dörnberg, *Ölversorgung*, p. 29 f.
21. On the Torpedo Crisis cf. C. Bekker, *Verdammte See. Ein Kriegstagebuch der deutschen Marine* (Oldenburg 1971) pp. 113–32; K. Dönitz, *Zehn Jahre und zwanzig Tage* (Bonn 1958) pp. 86–99.
22. Domarus, *Hitler Reden, II*, p. 1315. In the same speech Hitler mentioned the sum of 90 thousand million Reichsmarks which had supposedly been spent on *Wehrmacht* armament since January 1933. Partly as a result of the unsatisfactory nature of the sources, especially in the case of the *Luftwaffe*, the investigation of this figure in various studies has led to divergent findings. These however suggest a total expenditure of in the region of 60 thousand million Reichsmarks on armaments alone as realistic. Cf. Volkmann, *NS-Wirtschaft*, p. 245 ff. On Navy expenditure, see above p. 81.
23. Cf. Vogelsang, *Dokumente*, p. 434 f.
24. On the armaments programmes see above pp. 29 ff. and 59 ff.
25. Cf. Thomas, *Wehr- und Rüstungswirtschaft*, p. 62 f.
26. Cf. above p. 61 f.
27. Cf. above p. 75 f.

28. Cf. Absolon, *Wehrmacht*, I, p. 233 f.; II, p. 450, p. 478; Meinck, *Aufrüstung*, p. 101 ff., espec. p. 113 ff.; Müller, *Heer*, p. 216 ff.; Rautenberg, *Rüstungspolitik*, p. 332 ff.

29. Cf. above p. 12 ff.

30. Cf. Volkmann, *NS-Wirtschaft*, p. 287 ff; Dülffer also points out the significance of Hitler's general demands to accelerate rearmament, in *Beginn des Krieges*, p. 456 f.

31. Cf. Thomas, *Wehr- und Rüstungswirtschaft*, and Part I in particular; cf. also Volkmann, *NS-Wirtschaft*, p. 229 ff.

32. Cf. Thomas, *Wehr- und Rüstungswirtschaft*, p. 89 ff. and 108 ff.

33. Proof of Blomberg's co-ordinating function in the armaments sector as postulated by Dülffer in *Beginn des Krieges*, p. 452 is inadequate; Dülffer by-passes the question and instead deals with the operative sector. Nevertheless Blomberg and Thomas did of course emphatically represent the overall, if unco-ordinated, demands of the *Wehrmacht* in economic circles.

34. Cf. Volkmann, *NS-Wirtschaft*, pp. 245 ff. and the contributions by W. A. Boelcke (p. 29 ff.), H.-E. Volkmann (p. 81 ff.) and T. W. Mason (p. 158 ff.) in Forstmeier and Volkmann, *Wirtschaft und Rüstung*.

35. Cf. K.-J. Müller, 'General Ludwig Beck. Ein General zwischen Wilhelminismus und Nationalsozialismus', in I. Geiss and B. J. Wendt (eds), *Deutschland in der Weltpolitik des 19. und 20. Jahrhunderts* (Düsseldorf, 1973) p. 518 f.

36. Cf. *IMT*, vol. 34, p. 734 ff. For an interpretation see Meinck, *Aufrüstung*, p. 127 ff.; Robertson, *Pre-War Policy*, p. 90 ff.; Müller, *Heer*, pp. 211 and 236 ff.; Dülffer, *Weisungen*, p. 651; Geyer, *Aufrüstung*, p. 429 ff.; a comprehensive interpretation from Beck's point of view is to be found in Müller, *Beck-Studien*, Chap. 5, which shows clearly the lack of realism in Beck's concept of 'an active military policy of revisionism while avoiding a great war', a concept which moreover recalls Tirpitz.

37. Cf. above p. 41 ff.

38. Colonel Hoßbach's notes, printed in *Akten zur deutschen auswärtigen Politik* (*ADAP*), D VII, p. 167 ff. Cf. also Müller, *Beck-Studien*, Chap. 5.

39. Text of the directive of 21 December 1937 in *ADAP*, D VII, p. 547 ff. Cf. Müller, *Heer*, p. 246 f.; Dülffer, *Weisungen*, p. 651 f.; the directive reflected exactly Beck's view, cf. Müller, *Beck-Studien*, Chap. 5/III.

40. Cf. Müller, *Heer*, p. 249 ff.; Reynolds, *Treason*, p. 104 ff.; cf. especially Müller's penetrating and convincing analysis in *Beck-Studien*, Chap. 5/III, Doc. No. 43.

41. Text of the directive in *IMT*, vol. 34, p. 485 f.; for an interpretation cf. Robertson, *Pre-War Policy*, pp. 60 and 89 f.; Müller, *Heer*, p. 211 ff.; Dülffer, *Weimar*, p. 318 f.; Geyer, *Aufrüstung*, p. 421 ff.; for an interpretation of Beck's opinion cf. Müller, *Beck-Studien*, Chap. 5/I, as well as Doc. Nos. 28–30 printed there.

42. Documents on the General Staff study tour 1938 in BA-MA Wi IF/5 1502. Cf. Müller, *Beck-Studien*, Chap. 6.

43. Cf. Hitler's directive of 30 May 1938 in: *IMT*, vol. 25, p. 433 ff.

44. Cf. on this the directives of 30 May 1938 (*IMT*, vol. 25, p. 433 ff.), 21 October 1938 (*IMT*, vol. 34, p. 477 ff.), 24 November 1938 (*IMT*, vol. 34, p. 481 ff.), 3–11 April 1939 (*IMT*, vol. 34, p. 380 ff.).

45. Cf. *IMT*, vol. 34, p. 456 ff.
46. Cf. M. Cooper, *The German Army 1933–45* (London, 1978) p. 113 ff., also Salewski, *Bewaffnete Macht*, p. 143 f.
47. Cf. especially La France et L'Allemagne 1932–1936. Communications présentées au Colloque franco-allemand tenu à Paris du 10 au 12 mars 1977, Editions du Centre Nationale de la Recherche Scientifique (Paris 1980). There was another german-french conference, held at Bonn in September 1978, which centered on the years 1936–1939. The communications will be published by the German Historical Institute, Paris.
48. S. Haffner, *Anmerkungen zu Hitler* (Munich, 1978) p. 67.

NOTES TO CHAPTER 7

1. Cf. above p. 26.
2. See especially the following: Eberhard Jäckel, *Hitlers Weltanschauung. Entwurf einer Herrschaft* (Tübingen, 1969); Karl Lange, 'Hitlers unbeachtete Maximen. "Mein Kampf" und die Öffentlichkeit', in *Geschichte und Gegenwart* (Stuttgart, Berlin, Cologne, Mainz, 1968); K. D. Bacher, *Die deutsche Diktatur. Entstehung, Struktur, Folgen des Nationalsozialismus* (Cologne, Berlin, 1969); also Wette, *Ideologien*, p. 31 ff.
3. Cf. Messerschmidt, *Außenpolitik*, p. 535 ff. (the function of war in Hitler's programme).
4. 'Hitlers Zweites Buch. Ein Dokument aus dem Jahre 1928.' Introduced and with a commentary by Gerhard L. Weinberg, with a preface by Hans Rothfels, in *Quellen und Darstellungen zur Zeitgeschichte*, 7 (Stuttgart, 1961).
5. Ibid., p. 46.
6. Ibid., p. 46 f.
7. Ibid., p. 47.
8. Ibid., p. 163.
9. Cf. the much quoted first volume in the series, *Das Deutsche Reich und der Zweite Weltkrieg: Ursachen und Voraussetzungen der deutschen Kriegspolitik*, especially its conclusions.
10. *Hitlers Zweites Buch*, p. 62.
11. Vogelsang, *Dokumente*, p. 434 f.
12. Cf. especially Müller, *Heer*, pp. 47 and 61 ff., Messerschmidt, *Wehrmacht*, p. 18 ff.
13. Cf. above p. 33.
14. Hitler's radio appeal of 1 February 1933 printed in: *Schulthess Europäischer Geschichtskalender*, 74 (1933) p. 36. On general economic problems cf. Volkmann, *NS-Wirtschaft*, p. 232 ff.
15. Extract from the minutes of the cabinet meeting of 8 February 1933 in: *Akten zur deutschen auswärtigen Politik (ADAP)* C 1, 1, pp. 34–6.
16. On this problem cf. Volkmann, *NS-Wirtschaft* and the wide bibliography it gives.
17. Cf. Thomas, *Wehr- und Rüstungswirtschaft*, p. 51 ff.
18. *Hitlers Zweites Buch*, p. 62.
19. Vogelsang, *Dokumente*, p. 435. On the foreign–political aspects of armaments policy cf. Messerschmidt, *Außenpolitik*, p. 571 ff.
20. Messerschmidt, *Außenpolitik*, p. 569 ff.; also Wollstein, *Revisionismus*, and Hans-

Adolf Jacobsen, *Die nationalsozialistische Außenpolitik 1933–1938* (Frankfurt a.M., Berlin, 1968).

21. Messerschmidt, *Außenpolitik*, p. 580 ff.
22. Wette, *Ideologien*, p. 113 ff.
23. Messerschmidt, *Außenpolitik*, p. 623 and the works he mentions.
24. Cf. especially Messerschmidt, *Außenpolitik*, p. 632 ff.
25. On the higher officer corps in general see Müller, *Heer*; on Beck see Müller, *Beck-Studien*.
26. This was at any rate the opinion of the well-informed American military attaché in Berlin. Cf. Deist, *Die deutsche Aufrüstung in amerikanischer Sicht*, p. 293.
27. Phrase used by Messerschmidt in *Wehrmacht*, p. 488.
28. E.g. Beck's attitude to the armed SS units. Cf. Reynolds, *Treason*, p. 48 ff.
29. S. Haffner, *Anmerkungen zu Hitler* (Munich, 1978) p. 59.
30. Cf. above p. 91 ff.
31. On the power structure of the NS régime cf. Messerschmidt' remarks in *Außenpolitik*, p. 535 and the corresponding note.
32. Cf. Messerschmidt, *Außenpolitik*, p. 632 and the works he mentions.
33. Volkmann, *NS-Wirtschaft*, p. 232 ff.
34. Ibid., p. 262 ff.
35. Cf. above p. 89 ff.
36. Cf. Volkmann, *NS-Wirtschaft*, p. 315 f. Major-General Thomas as early as 1934 considered the possibility of short wars 'to secure and extend the limited strength of our armaments economy'. Geyer, *Aüfrüstung*, p. 461 ff.
37. Cf. Mason, *Arbeiterklasse und Volksgmemeinschaft*, p. 164.
38. Cf. also Carr, *Rüstung, Wirtschaft und Politik*, p. 437 ff.
39. Messerschmidt, *Außenpolitik*, p. 665 ff.

Bibliography

The following titles are intended to acquaint the reader with the most recent literature on German military history covering the period 1926/7 to 1939. I have, therefore, included only a few studies of a more general nature since these are sufficiently dealt with in the bibliographies of the standard reference works, see, e.g. Karl Dietrich Erdmann, 'Die Zeit der Weltkriege', in B. Gebhardt, *Handbuch zur deutschen Geschichte*, 9th ed. vol. 4/1 and 2, (Stuttgart, 1973, 1976). In addition, one should consult the comprehensive guide to the appropriate literature in the *Bibliographie zur Zeitgeschichte* which has appeared since 1953 as a supplement to the *Vierteljahrshefte für Zeitgeschichte*. The extensive specialist literature on the subject of military–technical aspects has been sacrificed in this selection in favour of military–historical aspects. I would, therefore, mention the bibliographies in the *Handbuch zur deutschen Militärgeschichte*. Only a few titles have been selected from the wealth of memoirs and literature on the military resistance. A survey of articles on military history is given in the *War and Society Newsletter* which has appeared since 1975 as a supplement to *Militärgeschichtliche Mitteilungen*.

R. Absolon, 'Wehrgesetz und Wehrdienst 1933–1945. Das Personalwesen in der Wehrmacht', *Schriftenreihe des Bundesarchivs*, 5 (Boppard, 1960).

R. Absolon, 'Die Wehrmacht im Dritten Reich. Aufbau, Gliederung, Recht, Verwaltung', 3 vols, *Schriften des Bundesarchivs*, 16/ I–III (Boppard, 1963, 1971, 1975).

U. Albert, 'Die deutsche Wiederaufrüstung der Dreißiger Jahre als Teil der staatlichen Arbeitsbeschaffung und ihre Finanzierung durch das System der Mefowechsel', Diss. (Nuremberg, 1956).

R. Barthel, 'Theorie und Praxis der Heeresmotorisierung im faschistischen Deutschland bis 1939', Phil. Diss. (Leipzig, 1967).

R. Barthel, 'Rüstungswirtschaftliche Forderungen der Reichswehrführung im Juni 1934', *Zeitschrift für Militärgeschichte*, 9 (1970) pp. 83–92.

W. Baum, 'Die Reichswehr und das wehrpolitische Amt der Nationalsozialistischen Deutschen Arbeiterpartei', *Allgemeine Schweizerische Militärzeitschrift*, 6 (1965) pp. 345–51.

W. Baumgart, 'Zur Ansprache Hitlers vor den Führern der Wehrmacht am 22. August 1939', *Vierteljahrshefte für Zeitgeschichte*, 16 (1968) pp. 120–49.

H. Bennecke, *Hitler und die SA*, (Munich, 1962).

→ E. W. Bennett, *German Rearmament and the West, 1932–1933* (Princeton 1979).

J. Benoist-Méchin, *Geschichte der deutschen Militärmacht 1918–1946*, vols 1–4 (Oldenburg, Hamburg, 1965).

V. R. Berghahn, 'Das Ende des "Stahlhelms"', *Vierteljahrshefte für Zeitgeschichte*, 13 (1965) pp. 446–51.

V. R. Berghahn, 'Der Stahlhelm. Bund der Frontsoldaten 1918–1935', *Beiträge zur Geschichte des Parlamentarismus und der politischen Parteien*, 33 (Düsseldorf, 1966).

V. R. Berghahn (ed.), *Militarismus, Neue Wissenschaftliche Bibliothek*, 83 (Cologne, 1975).

W. Bernhardt, *Die deutsche Aufrüstung 1934–1939. Militärische und politische Konzeptionen und ihre Einschätzung durch die Alliierten* (Frankfurt, 1969).

K. W. Bird, *Weimar, the German Naval Officer Corps and the Rise of National Socialism* (Amsterdam, 1977).

W. Birkenfeld, 'Der synthetische Treibstoff 1933–1945. Ein Beitrag zur nationalsozialistischen Wirtschafts- und Rüstungspolitik', *Studien und Dokumente zur Geschichte des Zweiten Weltkrieges*, 8 (Göttingen, Berlin, Frankfurt a.M., 1964).

Ch. Bloch, *Die SA und die Krise des NS-Regimes 1934* (Frankfurt a.M., 1970).

H. Boehm, 'Zur Ansprache Hitlers vor den Führern der Wehrmacht am 22. August 1939', *Vierteljahrshefte für Zeitgeschichte*, 19 (1971) pp. 294–300.

H. Boog, 'Die deutsche Luftwaffenführung 1935–1945. Generalstabsausbildung – Führungsprobleme – Spitzengliederung', *Beiträge zur Militär- und Kriegsgeschichte*, 21 (Stuttgart, 1980).

H. Boog, 'Das Offizierkorps der Luftwaffe 1935–1945', *Das deutsche Offizierkorps 1860–1960. Deutsche Führungsschichten der Neuzeit*, 11 (Boppard, 1980).

P. Bor, *Gespräche mit Halder* (Wiesbaden, 1950).

G. Botz, 'Die Eingliederung Österreichs in das Deutsche Reich. Planung und Verwirklichung des politisch-administrativen Anschlusses (1938–1940)', *Schriftenreihe des Ludwig-Boltzmann-Instituts für Geschichte der Arbeiterbewegung*, vol. 1, 2nd ed. (Vienna, Zürich, Munich, 1976).

K. D. Bracher and W. Sauer and G. Schulz, 'Die nationalsozialistische Machtergreifung. Studien zur Errichtung des totalitären Herrschaftssystems in Deutschland 1933/34', *Schriften des Instituts für politische Wissenschaft*, vol. 14, 2nd ed. (Cologne und Opladen, 1962).

K. D. Bracher, *Die Auflösung der Weimarer Republik. Eine Studie zum Problem des Machtverfalls in der Demokratie*, 4th ed. (Villingen, 1964).

M. Braubach, 'Der Einmarsch deutscher Truppen in die entmilitarisierte Zone am Rhein im März 1936. Ein Beitrag zur Vorgeschichte des zweiten Weltkrieges', *Arbeitsgemeinschaft für Forschung des Landes Nordrhein-Westfalen, Geisteswissenschaften*, 54 (Cologne, Opladen, 1956).

G. Breit, 'Das Staats- und Gesellschaftsbild deutscher Generale beider Weltkriege im Spiegel ihrer Memoiren', *Militärgeschichtliche Studien*, 17 (Boppard, 1973).

M. Broszat, 'Der Staat Hitlers. Grundlegung und Entwicklung seiner inneren Verfassung', *dtv-Weltgeschichte des 20. Jahrhunderts*, 9, 3rd ed. (Munich, 1973).

P. Bucher, 'Der Reichswehrprozeß. Der Hochverrat der Ulmer Reichswehroffiziere 1929/30', *Militärgeschichtliche Studien*, 4 (Boppard, 1967).

H. Buchheim and M. Broszat and H. A. Jacobsen and H. Krausnick, *Anatomie des SS-Staates*, 2 vols (Olten and Freiburg, 1965).

H. Bullock, *Hitler. A Study in Tyranny*. Rev. ed. (New York, 1962).

W. Bußmann, 'Zur Entstehung und Überlieferung der "Hoßbach-Niederschrift"', *Vierteljahrshefte für Zeitgeschichte*, 16 (1968) pp. 373–84.

W. Carr, *Arms, Autarky and Aggression. A Study in German Foreign Policy 1933–1939* (London, 1972).

W. Carr, 'Rüstung, Wirtschaft und Politik am Vorabend des Zweiten Weltkrieges', in W. Michalka (ed.), *Nationalsozialistische Außenpolitik, Wege der Forschung*, 297 (Darmstadt, 1978) pp. 437–54.

B. A. Carroll, 'Design for Total War. Arms and Economics in the Third Reich', *Studies in European History*, 17 (The Hague, Paris, 1968).

F. L. Carsten, *The Reichswehr and Politics, 1918 to 1933* (Berkeley, 1973).

G. Castellan, *Le Réarmement Claudestin du Reich 1933–1935* (Paris, 1954).

M. Cooper, *The German Army 1933–1945. Its political and military failure* (London, 1978).

A. Craig, *The Politics of the Prussian Army 1640–1945* (Oxford, 1955).

W. Deist, 'Internationale und nationale Aspekte der Abrüstungsfrage 1924–1932', in H. Rößler (ed.), *Locarno und die Weltpolitik 1924–1932* (Göttingen, 1969) pp. 64–93.

W. Deist, 'De Gaulle et Guderian. L'influence des expériences militaires de la première guerre mondiale en France et en Allemagne', *Etudes Gaulliennes*, V (1977) Nr. 17, pp. 47–57.

W. Deist, Zum Problem der deutschen Aufrüstung 1933–1936, in *Francia. Forschungen zur westeuropäischen Geschichte*, 5 (1977) pp. 539–565.

W. Deist, 'Die deutsche Aufrüstung in amerikanischer Sicht. Berichte des US-Militärattachés in Berlin aus den Jahren 1933–1939,' in *Rußland-Deutschland-Amerika, Frankfurter Historische Abhandlungen*, 17 (Wiesbaden, 1978) pp. 279–95.

K. Demeter, *Das deutsche Offizierkorps in Gesellschaft und Staat 1650–1945*, 4th rev. and enlarged ed. (Frankfurt, 1965).

C. Deutsch, *Hitler and his Generals. The Hidden Crisis, January–June 1938* (Minneapolis, 1974).

Das Deutsche Reich und der Zweite Weltkrieg, ed. Militärgeschichtliches Forschungsamt.

vol. 1. Ursachen und Voraussetzungen der deutschen Kriegspolitik.

W. Wette, Ideologien, Propaganda und Innenpolitik als Voraussetzungen der Kriegspolitik des Dritten Reiches;

H.-E. Volkmann, Die NS-Wirtschaft in Vorbereitung des Krieges;

W. Deist, Die Aufrüstung der Wehrmacht;

M. Messerschmidt, Außenpolitik und Kriegsvorbereitung (Stuttgart, 1979).

vol. 2. Die Errichtung der Hegemonie auf dem europäischen Kontinent (with contributions by K. A. Maier, H. Rohde, B. Stegemann and H. Umbreit) (Stuttgart, 1979).

Deutschland im zweiten Weltkrieg. vol. 1: Vorbereitung, Entfesselung und Verlauf des Krieges bis zum 22. Juni 1941. Von einem Autorenkollektiv unter der Leitung von G. Hass (Cologne, 1974).

K. Dönitz, *Zehn Jahre und zwanzig Tage*, 2nd ed. (Frankfurt, 1963).

M. Domarus, *Hitler. Reden und Proklamationen 1932–1945. Kommentiert von einem deutschen Zeitgenossen*, 2 vols (Würzburg, 1962–3).

A. Dorpalen, *Hindenburg in der Geschichte der Weimarer Republik* (Berlin, Frankfurt a.M., 1966).

J. Dülffer, 'Weisungen an die Wehrmacht als Ausdruck ihrer Gleichschaltung 1938/39', *Wehrwissenschaftliche Rundschau*, 18 (1968) pp. 651–5, 705–13.

J. Dülffer, 'Überlegungen von Kriegsmarine und Heer zur Wehrmachtspitzengliederung und zur Führung der Wehrmacht im Kriege im Februar-März 1938', *Militärgeschichtliche Mitteilungen*, 9 (1971) pp. 145–71.

J. Dülffer, *Weimar, Hitler und die Marine. Reichspolitik und Flottenbau 1920–1939. Mit einem Anhang von Jürgen Rohwer* (Düsseldorf, 1973).

J. Dülffer, 'Determinanten der deutschen Marine-Entwicklung in der Zwischenkriegszeit (1920–1939)', *Marine-Rundschau*, 72 (1975) pp. 8–19.

J. Dülffer, 'Der Beginn des Krieges 1939. Hitler, die innere Krise und das Mächtesystem', *Geschichte und Gesellschaft*, 2 (1976) pp. 443–70.

D. Eichholtz and W. Schumann (ed.), *Anatomie des Krieges. Neue Dokumente über die Rolle des deutschen Monopolkapitals bei der Vorbereitung und Durchführung des zweiten Weltkrieges* (East Berlin, 1969).

J. T. Emmerson, *The Rhineland Crisis, 7. March 1936. A study on multilateral diplomacy* (London, 1977).

A. Faust, 'Der Nationalsozialistische Studentenbund. Studenten und Nationalsozialismus in der Weimarer Republik', 2 vols *Geschichte und Gesellschaft. Bochumer historische Studien* (Düsseldorf, 1973).

D. Fensch and O. Groehler, 'Imperialistische Ökonomie und militärische Strategie. Eine Denkschrift Wilhelm Groeners', *Zeitschrift für Geschichtswissenschaft*, 19 (1971) pp. 1167–77.

J. Fest, *Hitler. Eine Biographie* (Frankfurt a.M., 1973).

G. Förster, 'Totaler Krieg und Blitzkrieg. Die Theorie des totalen Krieges und des Blitzkrieges in der Militärdoktrin des faschis-

tischen Deutschlands am Vorabend des Zweiten Weltkrieges',
Militärhistorische Studien, N.F. 10 (East Berlin, 1967).

O. W. Förster, 'Das Befestigungswesen. Rückblick und Ausschau',
Wehrmacht im Kampf, 25 (Neckargemünd, 1960).

W. Foerster, *Generaloberst Ludwig Beck. Sein Kampf gegen den Krieg.
Aus nachgelassenen Papieren des Generalstabschefs*, 2nd ed.
(Munich, 1953).

F. Forstmeier and H.-E. Volkmann (ed.), *Wirtschaft und Rüstung am
Vorabend des Zweiten Weltkrieges* (Düsseldorf, 1975).

M. Freund (ed.), 'Geschichte des Zweiten Weltkrieges in
Dokumenten', vols 1–3, *Weltgeschichte der Gegenwart in Dokumenten* (Freiburg/Munich, 1953/6).

H.-W. Gatzke, *Stresemann and the Rearmament of Germany* (Baltimore,
1954).

C.-A. Gemzell, 'Raeder, Hitler und Skandinavien. Der Kampf für
einen maritimen Operationsplan', *Bibliotheca Historica Ludensis*,
16 (Lund, 1965).

C.-A. Gemzell, 'Organization, Conflict and Innovation: A Study of
German Naval Strategic Planning 1888–1940', *Lund-Studies in
International History*, 4 (Lund, 1973).

'Die Generalstäbe in Deutschland 1871 bis 1945. Aufgaben in der
Armee und Stellung im Staate.-Die Entwicklung der militäri-
schen Luftfahrt in Deutschland 1920 bis 1933. Planung und
Maßnahmen zur Schaffung einer Fliegertruppe in der
Reichswehr', *Beiträge zur Militär- und Kriegsgeschichte*, 2
(Stuttgart, 1962).

O. Geßler, 'Reichswehrpolitik in der Weimarer Zeit', Kurt
Sendtner (ed.), (Stuttgart, 1958).

M. Geyer, 'Die Landesverteidigung. Wehrstruktur am Ende der
Weimarer Republik' Staatsexamensarbeit (Freiburg, 1972).

M Geyer, 'Die Wehrmacht der Deutschen Republik ist die
Reichswehr', *Militärgeschichtliche Mitteilungen*, 14 (1973) pp.
152–99.

M. Geyer, 'Das Zweite Rüstungsprogramm (1930–1934)', *Militärgeschichtliche Mitteilungen*, 17 (1975) pp. 125–72.

M. Geyer, 'Militär, Rüstung und Außenpolitik – Aspekte militär-
ischer Revisionspolitik in der Zwischenkriegszeit', in M. Funke
(ed.), *Hitler, Deutschland und die Mächte. Materialien zur
Außenpolitik des Dritten Reiches* (Düsseldorf, 1976) pp. 239–68.

M. Geyer, *Aufrüstung oder Sicherheit. Die Reichswehr in der Krise der
Machtpolitik 1924–1936* (Wiesbaden, 1980).

L. Baron Geyr v. Schweppenburg, *The Critical Years* (London, 1952).

W. Görlitz, *Model. Strategie der Defensive*, 2nd ed. (Wiesbaden, 1975).

W. Görlitz (ed.), *Generalfeldmarschall Keitel. Verbrecher oder Offizier? Erinnerungen, Briefe, Dokumente des Chefs OKW* (Göttingen, Berlin, Frankfurt a.M., 1961).

K. Gossweiler, 'Der Übergang von der Weltwirtschaftskrise zur Rüstungskonjunktur in Deutschland 1933 bis 1934. Ein historischer Beitrag zur Problematik staatsmonopolistischer "Krisenüberwindung"', *Jahrbuch für Wirtschaftsgeschichte* (1966/II) pp. 55–116.

D. Groener-Geyer, *General Groener. Soldat und Staatsmann* (Frankfurt a.M., 1955).

P. Gschaider, 'Das österreichische Bundesheer 1938 und seine Überführung in die Deutsche Wehrmacht', Phil. Diss. (Vienna, 1967).

H. Guderian, *Erinnerungen eines Soldaten* (Heidelberg, 1951).

K. Gundelach, 'Gedanken über die Führung eines Luftkrieges gegen England bei der Luftflotte 2. in den Jahren 1938/39', *Wehrwissenschaftliche Rundschau*, 10 (1960) pp. 33–46.

S. Haffner, *Anmerkungen zu Hitler* 5th ed. (Munich, 1978).

Generaloberst Halder, 'Kriegstagebuch. Tägliche Aufzeichnungen des Chefs des Generalstabes des Heeres 1939–1942', H.-A. Jacobsen and A. Philippi (ed.), vol. 1: Vom Polenfeldzug bis zum Ende der Westoffensive (14.8.1939–30.6.1940), (Stuttgart, 1962).

G. W. F. Hallgarten, *Hitler, Reichswehr und Industrie. Zur Geschichte der Jahre 1918–1933*, 2nd ed. (Frankfurt a.M., 1955).

Handbuch zur deutschen Militärgeschichte 1648–1939, ed. Militärgeschichtliches Forschungsamt.

Abschn. VI. *Reichswehr und Republik (1918–1933)* R. Wohlfeil, Heer und Republik; E. Graf v. Matuschka, Organisation des Reichsheeres (Frankfurt, 1970).

Abschn. VII. *Wehrmacht und Nationalsozialismus 1933–1939* M. Salewski, Die bewaffnete Macht im Dritten Reich 1933–1939; Herbert Schottelius and Gustav-Adolf Caspar, Die Organisation des Heeres 1933–1939; Rolf Güth et al., Die Organisation der Kriegsmarine bis 1939; Karl Köhler and Karl-Heinz Hummel, Die Organisation der Luftwaffe 1933–1939 (Munich, 1979).

Abschn. VIII. *Deutsche Marinegeschichte der Neuzeit* W. Petter, Deutsche Flottenrüstung von Wallenstein bis Tirpitz;

R. Güth, Die Organisation der deutschen Marine in Krieg und Frieden 1913–1933; J. Dülffer, Die Reichs- und Kriegsmarine 1918–1939 (Munich, 1977).

E. W. Hansen, 'Reichswehr und Industrie. Rüstungswirtschaftliche Zusammenarbeit und wirtschaftliche Mobilmachungsvorbereitungen 1923–1932', *Militärgeschichtliche Studien*, 24 (Boppard, 1978).

B. Heimann and J. Schunke, 'Eine geheime Denkschrift zur Luftkriegskonzeption Hitler-Deutschlands vom Mai 1933', *Zeitschrift für Militärgeschichte*, 3 (1964) pp. 72–86.

E. Hennig, 'Industrie, Aufrüstung und Kriegsvorbereitung im deutschen Faschismus (1933–1939). Anmerkungen zum Stand 'der' neueren Faschismusdiskussion', *Gesellschaftliche Beiträge zur Marxschen Theorie*, 5 (Frankfurt a.M., 1975) pp. 68–148.

G. Henrikson, 'Das Nürnberger Dokument 386–PS (Das "Hoßbach-Protokoll")', in *Probleme deutscher Zeitgeschichte. Lund-Studies in International History*, 2 (Stockholm, 1971) pp. 151–94.

H. Herzfeld, 'Politik, Heer und Rüstung in der Zwischenkriegszeit', *Ausgewählte Aufsätze. Dargebracht als Festgabe zum siebzigsten Geburtstage von seinen Freunden und Schülern* (Berlin, 1962) pp. 255–77.

K. Hildebrand, *The Foreign Policy of the Third Reich* (London, 1973).

F. Frhr. Hiller v. Gaertringen, 'Groener', *Neue deutsche Biographie*, vol. VII (Berlin, 1966) pp. 111–14.

A. Hillgruber, 'Quellen und Quellenkritik zur Vorgeschichte des Zweiten Weltkrieges', *Wehrwissenschaftliche Rundschau*, 14 (1964) pp. 110–26.

A. Hillgruber, 'Deutschlands Rolle in der Vorgeschichte der beiden Weltkriege', *Die deutsche Frage in der Welt*, 7 (Göttingen, 1967).

A. Hillgruber, 'Der Zweite Weltkrieg, 1939–1945', in D. Geyer (ed.), *Osteuropa-Handbuch, Sowjetunion. Außenpolitik 1917–1955* (Cologne, Vienna, (1972) pp. 270–342.

A. Hillgruber, *Großmachtpolitik und Militarismus im 20. Jahrhundert. 3 Beiträge zum Kontinuitätsproblem* (Düsseldorf, 1974).

H. Höhne, *Der Orden unter dem Totenkopf. Die Geschichte der SS* (Frankfurt, 1969).

H. Höhne, *Canaris. Patriot im Zwielicht* (Munich, 1976).

E. L. Homze, *Arming the Luftwaffe. The Reich Air Ministry and the German aircraft industry 1919–39* (Lincoln, 1976).

F. Hoßbach, *Zwischen Wehrmacht und Hitler*, 2nd ed. (Wolfenbüttel-Hannover, 1965).

W. Hubatsch (ed.), *Hitlers Weisungen für die Kriegführung 1939–1945. Dokumente des Oberkommandos der Wehrmacht* (Frankfurt a.M., 1962).

International Military Tribunal. *Trial of the Major War Criminals before the International Military Tribunal, 14 November 1945–1 October 1946*, 42 vols (Nuremberg, 1947–9).

D. J. C. Irving, *The rise and fall of the Luftwaffe. The Life of Luftwaffe Marshall Erich Milch* (London, 1973).

H. A. Jacobsen, *Der Zweite Weltkrieg. Grundzüge der Politik und Strategie in Dokumenten* (Frankfurt a.M., 1965).

H. A. Jacobsen, 'Krieg in Theorie und Praxis des National-sozialismus', *Vom alten zum neuen Österreich. Festschrift für L. Jedlicka* (Vienna, 1976).

O. Jacobsen, *Erich Marcks. Soldat und Gelehrter* (Göttingen, Frankfurt a.M., Zürich, 1971).

E. Jäckel, *Hitlers Weltanschauung. Entwurf einer Herrschaft* (Tübingen, 1969).

M. H. Kater, 'Ansätze zu einer Soziologie der SA bis zur Röhm-Krise', in U. Engelhardt and V. Sellin and H. Stuke (ed.), *Soziale Bewegung und politische Verfassung. Beiträge zur Geschichte der modernen Welt* (Stuttgart, 1976) pp. 798–831.

M. Kehrig, 'Die Wiedereinrichtung des deutschen militärischen Attaché-Dienstes nach dem Ersten Weltkrieg (1919–1933)', *Militärgeschichtliche Studien*, 2 (Boppard, 1966).

K. Kens and H. J. Nowarra, *Die deutschen Flugzeuge 1933–1945*, 2nd ed. (Munich, 1964).

Graf J. A. Kielmansegg, *Der Fritsch-Prozeß 1938. Ablauf und Hintergründe* (Hamburg, 1949).

Burton H. Klein, *Germany's Economic Preparations for War* (Harvard, Harvard University Press, 1959).

K.-G. Klietmann, *Die Waffen-SS. Eine Dokumentation* (Osnabrück, 1965).

K. Köhler, 'Douhet und Douhetismus', *Wehrwissenschaftliche Rundschau*, 14 (1964) pp. 88–91.

K. Köhler, 'Operativer Luftkrieg. Eine Wortbildung zur Bezeichnung unterschiedlicher Vorstellungen', *Wehrkunde*, 16 (1967) pp. 265–9.

General Ernst Köstring, 'Der militärische Mittler zwischen dem

Deutschen Reich und der Sowjetunion 1921–1941', H. Teske (ed.), (Frankfurt a.M., 1966).

H. v. Kotze (ed.), 'Heeresadjutant bei Hitler 1938–1943. Aufzeichnungen des Majors Engel', *Schriftenreihe der Vierteljahrshefte für Zeitgeschichte*, 29 (Stuttgart, 1974).

H. Krausnick, 'Vorgeschichte und Beginn des militärischen Widerstandes gegen Hitler', in *Die Vollmacht des Gewissens*, vol. 1 (Munich, 1955) pp. 175–380.

H. Krausnick and H. C. Deutsch et al. (ed.), 'H. Groscurth. Tagebücher eines Abwehroffiziers 1938–1940' *Quellen und Darstellungen zur Zeitgeschichte*, 19 (Stuttgart, 1970).

A. Kuhn, 'Hitlers außenpolitisches Programm. Entstehung und Entwicklung 1919–1933', *Stuttgarter Beiträge zur Geschichte und Politik*, 5 (Stuttgart, 1970).

A. Kuhn, *Das faschistische Herrschaftssystem und die moderne Gesellschaft* (Hamburg, 1973).

E. Ludendorff, *Der totale Krieg* (Munich, 1935).

K.-H. Ludwig, *Technik und Ingenieure im Dritten Reich* (Düsseldorf, 1974).

K. J. Macksey, *Guderian. Panzer-General* (London, 1975).

K. A. Maier, 'Guernica, 26.4.1937. Die deutsche Intervention und der "Fall Guernica"', *Einzelschriften zur militärischen Geschichte des Zweiten Weltkrieges*, 17 (Freiburg, 1975).

E. v. Manstein, *Aus einem Soldatenleben 1887–1939* (Bonn, 1958).

T. W. Mason, 'Arbeiterklasse und Volksgemeinschaft. Dokumente und Materialien zur Deutschen Arbeiterpolitik 1936–1939', *Schriften des Zentralinstituts für sozialwissenschaftliche Forschung der Freien Universität Berlin*, 22 (Opladen, 1975).

T. W. Mason, *Sozialpolitik im Dritten Reich, Arbeiterklasse und Volksgemeinschaft* (Opladen, 1977).

W. Meier-Dörnberg, 'Die Ölversorgung der Kriegsmarine 1935 bis 1945', *Einzelschriften zur militärischen Geschichte des Zweiten Weltkrieges*, 11 (Freiburg, 1973).

H. Meier-Welcker, *Seeckt* (Frankfurt a.M., 1967).

H. Meier-Welcker, 'Aus dem Briefwechsel zweier junger Offiziere des Reichsheeres 1930–1938', *Militärgeschichtliche Mitteilungen*, 14 (1973) pp. 57–100.

H. Meier-Welcker, 'Der Weg zum Offizier im Reichsheer der Weimarer Republik', *Militärgeschichtliche Mitteilungen*, 19 (1976) pp. 147–80.

G. Meinck, 'Der Reichsverteidigungsrat', *Wehrwissenschaftliche Rundschau*, 6 (1956) pp. 411–22.

G. Meinck, 'Hitler und die deutsche Aufrüstung 1933–1937', *Veröffentlichungen des Instituts für Europäische Geschichte Mainz*, 19 (Wiesbaden, 1959).

M. Messerschmidt, 'Aspekte der Militärseelsorgepolitik in nationalsozialistischer Zeit', *Militärgeschichtliche Mitteilungen*, 3 (1968) pp. 63–105.

M. Messerschmidt, 'Zur Militärseelsorgepolitik im Zweiten Weltkrieg', *Militärgeschichtliche Mitteilungen*, 5 (1969) pp. 37–85.

M. Messerschmidt, *Die Wehrmacht im NS-Staat. Zeit der Indoktrination* (Hamburg, 1969).

M. Messerschmidt, 'Revision, Neue Ordnung, Krieg. Akzente der Völkerrechtswissenschaft in Deutschland 1933 bis 1945', *Militärgeschichtliche Mitteilungen*, 9 (1971) pp. 61–95.

G. Meyer, 'Generalfeldmarschall Wilhelm Ritter v. Leeb. Tagebuchaufzeichnungen und Lagebeurteilungen aus zwei Weltkriegen', *Beiträge zur Militär- und Kriegsgeschichte*, 16 (Stuttgart, 1976).

A. S. Milward, 'Die deutsche Kriegswirtschaft 1939–1945', *Schriftenreihe der Vierteljahrshefte für Zeitgeschichte*, 12 (Stuttgart, 1966).

H. Model, *Der deutsche Generalstabsoffizier. Seine Auswahl und Ausbildung in Reichswehr, Wehrmacht und Bundeswehr* (Frankfurt a.M., 1968).

K.-J. Müller, 'Reichswehr und "Röhm-Affäre". Aus den Akten des Wehrkreiskommandos (Bayer.) VII', *Militärgeschichtliche Mitteilungen*, 3(1968) pp. 107–44.

K.-J. Müller, 'Das Heer und Hitler. Armee und nationalsozialistisches Regime 1933–1940', *Beiträge zur Militär- und Kriegsgeschichte*, 10 (Stuttgart, 1969).

K.-J. Müller, 'Ludwig Beck. Probleme seiner Biographie', *Militärgeschichtliche Mitteilungen*, 11 (1972) pp. 167–75.

K.-J. Müller, 'Staat und Politik im Denken Ludwig Becks', *Historische Zeitschrift*, 215 (1972) pp. 607–31.

K.-J. Müller and E. Opitz (ed.), *Militär und Militarismus in der Weimarer Republik* (Düsseldorf, 1978).

K.-J. Müller, *Armee, Politik und Gesellschaft in Deutschland 1933–1945. Studien zum Verhältnis von Armee und NS-System* (Paderborn, 1979).

K.-J. Müller, 'General Ludwig Beck. Studien und Dokumente zur Tätigkeit und Vorstellungswelt des Generalstabschefs des deutschen Heeres 1933–1938', *Schriftenreihe des Bundesarchivs* (Boppard, 1980).

B. Mueller-Hillebrand, *Das Heer 1933–1945. Entwicklung des organisatorischen Aufbaues*, vol. 1: *Das Heer bis zum Kriegsbeginn* (Darmstadt, 1954).

W. Murray, 'The Change in the European Balance of Power, 1938–1939', Diss. (Yale, 1975).

W. Murray, 'German Air Power and the Munich Crisis', *War and Society*, 2 (1977) pp. 107–18.

W. K. Nehring, *Die Geschichte der deutschen Panzerwaffe 1916 bis 1945* (Berlin, 1969).

G. Niedhart (ed.), 'Kriegsbeginn 1939. Entfesselung oder Ausbruch des Zweiten Weltkrieges?', *Wege der Forschung*, 374 (Darmstadt, 1976).

'Offiziere im Bild von Dokumenten aus drei Jahrhunderten', *Beiträge zur Militär- und Kriegsgeschichte*, 6 (Stuttgart, 1964).

R. J. O'Neill, *The German Army and the Nazi Party 1933–1939* (London, 1966).

R. J. Overy, 'The German Pre-war Aircraft Production Plans: November 1936 – April 1939', *The English Historical Review*, 90 (1975) pp. 778–97.

D. Petzina, 'Die Mobilisierung deutscher Arbeitskräfte vor und während des Zweiten Weltkrieges', *Vierteljahrshefte für Zeitgeschichte*, 18 (1970) pp. 443–55.

D. Petzina, 'Autarkiepolitik im Dritten Reich. Der nationalsozialistische Vierjahresplan (1936–1942)', *Schriftenreihe der Vierteljahrshefte für Zeitgeschichte*, 16 (Stuttgart, 1968).

G. Post jr, *The Civil-Military Fabric of Weimar Foreign Policy* (Princeton, 1973).

K. Prümm, *Die Literatur des Soldatischen Nationalismus der 20er Jahre (1918–1933). Gruppenideologie und Epochenproblematik*, 2 vols (Kronberg, 1974).

E. Raeder, *Mein Leben*, 2 vols (Tübingen, 1957).

W. Rahn, *Reichsmarine und Landesverteidigung 1919–1928. Konzeption und Führung der Marine in der Weimarer Republik* (Munich, 1976).

H.-J. Rautenberg, 'Deutsche Rüstungspolitik vom Beginn der Genfer Abrüstungskonferenz bis zur Wiedereinführung der allgemeinen Wehrpflicht 1932–1935', Phil. Diss. (Bonn, 1973).

H.-J. Rautenberg, 'Drei Dokumente zur Planung eines 300,000 Mann-Friedensheeres aus dem Dezember 1933', *Militärgeschichtliche Mitteilungen*, 22 (1977) pp. 103–39.

N. Reynolds, *Treason was no crime* (London, 1976).

E. M. Robertson, 'Zur Wiederbesetzung des Rheinlandes 1936', *Vierteljahrshefte für Zeitgeschichte*, 10 (1962) pp. 178–205.

E. M. Robertson, *Hitler's Pre-War Policy and Military Plans 1933–1939* (London, 1963).

E. M. Robertson (ed.), *The Origins of the Second World War. Historical interpretations* (London, 1971).

H. Rohde, 'Das deutsche Wehrmachttransportwesen im Zweiten Weltkrieg. Entstehung – Organisation – Aufgaben', *Beiträge zur Militär- und Kriegsgeschichte*, 12 (Stuttgart, 1971).

K. Rohe, 'Das Reichsbanner Schwarz Rot Gold. Ein Beitrag zur Geschichte und Struktur der politischen Kampfverbände zur Zeit der Weimarer Republik, *Beiträge zur Geschichte des Parlamentarismus und der politischen Parteien*, 34 (Düsseldorf, 1966).

H. Rosinski, *The German Army* (New York, 1966).

M. Salewski, *Entwaffnung und Militärkontrolle in Deutschland 1919–1927* (Munich, 1966).

M. Salewski, 'Selbstverständnis und historisches Bewußtsein der deutschen Kriegsmarine', *Marine-Rundschau*, 67 (1970) pp. 65–88.

M. Salewski, *Die deutsche Seekriegsleitung 1935–1945*, 3 vols (Frankfurt a.M., 1970, 1973, 1975).

M. Salewski, 'Marineleitung und politische Führung 1931–1935', *Militärgeschichtliche Mitteilungen*, 11 (1971) pp. 113–58.

M. Salewski, 'Zur deutschen Sicherheitspolitik in der Spätzeit der Weimarer Republik', *Vierteljahrshefte für Zeitgeschichte*, 22 (1974) pp. 121–47.

M. Salewski, 'England, Hitler und die Marine', in O. Franz (ed.), *Vom Sinn der Geschichte* (Stuttgart, 1976) pp. 163–84.

G. Sandhofer, 'Dokumente zum militärischen Werdegang des Großadmirals Dönitz', *Militärgeschichtliche Mitteilungen*, 1 (1967) pp. 59–81.

G. Sandhofer, 'Das Panzerschiff "A" und die Vorentwürfe von 1920 bis 1928', *Militärgeschichtliche Mitteilungen*, 3 (1968) pp. 35–62.

H. Gräfin Schall-Riaucour, *Aufstand und Gehorsam. Offizierstum und Generalstab im Umbruch. Leben und Wirken von Generaloberst Franz*

Halder, Generalstabschef 1938–1942 (Wiesbaden, 1972).

N. Schausberger, 'Wirtschaftliche Aspekte des Anschlusses Österreichs an das Deutsche Reich', *Militärgeschichtliche Mitteilungen*, 8 (1970) pp. 133–65.

N. Schausberger, *Rüstung in Österreich 1938–1945. Eine Studie über die Wechselwirkungen von Wirtschaft, Politik und Kriegführung* (Vienna, 1970).

D. Schoenbaum, *Hitler's social revolution – Class and status in Nazi Germany 1933–1939* (London, 1967).

G. Schreiber, 'Revisionismus und Weltmachtstreben. Marineführung und deutsch-italienische Beziehungen 1919 bis 1944', *Beiträge zur Militär- und Kriegsgeschichte*, 20 (Stuttgart, 1978).

G. Schreiber, 'Reichsmarine, Revisionismus und Weltmachtstreben', in K.-J. Müller and E. Opitz (ed.), *Militär und Militarismus in der Weimarer Republik* (Düsseldorf, 1978), pp. 149–76.

G. Schreiber, 'Zur Kontinuität des Groß- und Weltmachtstrebens der deutschen Marineführung', in *Militärgeschichtliche Mitteilungen*, 26 (1979) pp. 101–171.

K. Schützle, *Reichswehr wider die Nation. Zur Rolle der Reichswehr bei der Vorbereitung und Errichtung der faschistischen Diktatur in Deutschland (1929–1933)* (East Berlin, 1963).

G. Schulz, *Aufstieg des Nationalsozialismus. Krise und Revolution in Deutschland* (Frankfurt a.M., Berlin, Vienna, 1975).

W. Schumann and L. Nestler (ed.), *Weltherrschaft im Visier. Dokumente zu den Europa- und Weltherrschaftsplänen des deutschen Imperialismus von der Jahrhundertwende bis Mai 1945* (East Berlin, 1975).

K. G. P. Schuster, 'Der Rote Frontkämpferbund 1924–1929. Beiträge zur Geschichte und Organisationsstruktur eines politischen Kampfbundes', *Beiträge zur Geschichte des Parlamentarismus und der politischen Parteien*, 55 (Düsseldorf, 1975).

A. Schweitzer, 'Die wirtschaftliche Wiederaufrüstung Deutschlands von 1934–1936', *Zeitschrift für die gesamte Staatswissenschaft*, 114 (1958) pp. 594–637.

H. Senff, *Die Entwicklung der Panzerwaffe im deutschen Heer zwischen den beiden Weltkriegen. Eine Untersuchung der Auffassungen über ihren Einsatz an Hand von Vorschriften, literarischer Diskussion und tatsächlichem Heeresaufbau* (Frankfurt a.M., 1969).

F. M. v. Senger und Etterlin, *Die Kampfpanzer von 1916–1966*, 2nd ed. (Munich, 1971).

C. Siewert, *Schuldig? Die Generale unter Hitler. Stellung und Einfluss der hohen militärischen Führer im nationalsozialistischen Staat. Das Maß ihrer Verantwortung und Schuld* (Bad Nauheim, 1968).

B. F. Smith and A. F. Peterson (ed.), *Heinrich Himmler. Geheimreden 1933 bis 1945 und andere Ansprachen*, with an introduction by J. C. Fest (Frankfurt a.M., Berlin, Vienna, 1974).

H. Speidel (ed.), *Ludwig Beck, Studien* (Stuttgart, 1955).

Staat und NSDAP 1930–1932. Quellen zur Ära Brüning, eingel. von G. Schulz, bearb. von I. Meurer und U. Wengst, *Quellen zur Geschichte des Parlamentarismus und der politischen Parteien, 3. Reihe: Die Weimarer Republik, 3* (Düsseldorf, 1977).

J. Stelzner, 'Arbeitsbeschaffung und Wiederaufrüstung 1933–1936. Nationalsozialistische Beschäftigungspolitik und Aufbau der Wehr-und Rüstungswirtschaft', Diss. (Tübingen, Bamberg, 1976).

R. Stumpf, 'Die Luftwaffe als drittes Heer. Die Luftwaffen-Erdkampfverbände und das Problem der Sonderheere 1933 bis 1945', in U. Engelhardt and V. Sellin and H. Stuke (eds), *Soziale Bewegung und politische Verfassung Beiträge zur geschichte der modernen Welt* (Stuttgart, 1976) pp. 857–94.

J. Sywottek, 'Mobilmachung für den totalen Krieg. Die propagandistische Vorbereitung der deutschen Bevölkerung auf den Zweiten Weltkrieg', *Studien zur modernen Geschichte*, 18 (Opladen, 1976).

A. J. P. Taylor, *The Origins of the Second World War* (London, Penguin, 1964).

G. Tessin, *Deutsche Verbände und Truppen 1918–1939. Altes Heer, Freiwilligenverbände, Reichswehr, Heer, Luftwaffe, Landespolizei* (Osnabrück, 1974).

G. Thomas, 'Geschichte der deutschen Wehr- und Rüstungswirtschaft (1918–1943/45)', *Schriften des Bundesarchivs*, 14 (Boppard, 1966).

W. Treue, 'Hitlers Denkschrift zum Vierjahresplan 1936', *Vierteljahrshefte für Zeitgeschichte*, 3 (1955) pp. 184–210.

G. Ueberschär, 'Generaloberst Halder im militärischen Widerstand 1938–1940', *Wehrforschung*, 2 (1973) pp. 20–31.

H. Umbreit, 'Deutsche Militärverwaltungen 1938/39. Die militärische Besetzung der Tschechoslowakei und Polens', *Beiträge zur Militär und Kriegsgeschichte*, 18 (Stuttgart, 1977).

'Untersuchungen zur Geschichte des Offizierkorps. Anciennität und Beförderung nach Leistung', *Beiträge zur Militär- und Kriegsgeschichte*, 4 (Stuttgart, 1962).

P. Vauthier, *Die Kriegslehre des Generals Douhet* (Berlin, 1935).

K.-H. Völker, 'Die deutsche Luftwaffe 1933–1939. Aufbau, Führung und Rüstung der Luftwaffe sowie die Entwicklung der deutschen Luftkriegstheorie', *Beiträge zur Militär- und Kriegsgeschichte*, 8 (Stuttgart, 1967).

K.-H.Völker, 'Dokumente und Dokumentarfotos zur Geschichte der deutschen Luftwaffe. Aus den Geheimakten des Reichswehrministeriums 1919–1933 und des Reichsluftfahrtministeriums 1933–1939', *Beiträge zur Militär- und Kriegsgeschichte*, 9 (Stuttgart, 1968).

T. Vogelsang, 'Neue Dokumente zur Geschichte der Reichswehr 1930–1933', *Vierteljahrshefte für Zeitgeschichte*, 2 (1954) pp. 397–436.

T. Vogelsang, 'Reichswehr, Staat und NSDAP. Beiträge zur deutschen Geschichte 1930–32', *Quellen und Darstellungen zur Zeitgeschichte*, 11 (Stuttgart, 1962).

T. Vogelsang, 'Kurt von Schleicher. Ein General als Politiker', *Persönlichkeit und Geschichte*, 39 (Göttingen, 1965).

M. Vogt, 'Das Kabinett Müller II (1928–1930)', 2 vols, *Akten der Reichskanzlei, Weimarer Republik* (Boppard, 1970).

H.-E. Volkmann, 'Zur Interdependenz von Politik, Wirtschaft und Rüstung im NS-Staat', *Militärgeschichtliche Mitteilungen*, 15 (1974) pp. 161–72.

H.-E. Volkmann, 'Politik, Wirtschaft und Aufrüstung unter dem Nationalsozialismus', in M. Funke (ed.), *Hitler, Deutschland und die Mächte. Materialien zur Außenpolitik des Dritten Reiches* (Düsseldorf, 1976) pp. 269–91.

W. Wacker, 'Der Bau des Panzerschiffs "A" und der Reichstag', *Tübinger Studien zur Geschichte und Politik*, 11 (Tübingen, 1959).

E. Wagner (ed.), *Der General-Quartiermeister, Briefe und Tagebuchaufzeichnungen des Generalquartiermeisters des Heeres General der Artillerie Eduard Wagner* (Munich, Vienna, 1963).

G. Wagner (ed.), *Lagevorträge des Oberbefehlshabers der Kriegsmarine vor Hitler 1939–1945* (Munich, 1972).

R. Wagner, 'Die Wehrmachtführung und die Vierjahresplanpolitik im faschistischen Deutschland vor der Entfesselung des zweiten Weltkrieges', *Militärgeschichte*, 12 (1973) pp. 180–8.

K. J. Walde, *Guderian* (Frankfurt a.M., 1976).

J. L. Wallach, *Das Dogma der Vernichtungsschlacht. Die Lehren von Clausewitz und Schlieffen und ihre Wirkungen in zwei Weltkriegen* (Frankfurt a.M., 1967).

W. Warlimont, *Inside Hitler's Headquarters 1939–1945* (New York, 1964).

D. C. Watt, 'German Plans for the Reoccupation of the Rhineland. A note, *Journal of Contemporary History*, 1 (1966) pp. 193–9.

D. C. Watt, *Too serious a business. European armed forces and the approach to the Second World War* (London, 1975).

B. Wegner, 'Die Garde des "Führers" und die "Feuerwehr" der Ostfront. Zur neueren Literatur über die Waffen-SS', *Militärgeschichtliche Mitteilungen*, 23 (1978) pp. 210–36.

H. U. Wehler, 'Der Verfall der deutschen Kriegstheorie: Vom "Absoluten" zum "Totalen" Krieg oder von Clausewitz zu Ludendorff', in U. v. Gersdorff (ed.), *Geschichte und Militärgeschichte* (Frankfurt a.M., 1974) pp. 273–311.

J. W. Wheeler-Bennett, *Hindenburg. The Wooden Titan* (London, 1936).

J. W. Wheeler-Bennett, *Nemesis of Power. The German Army in Politics 1918–1945*, 2nd ed. (London, 1964).

N. Wiggershaus, 'Der deutsch-englische Flottenvertrag vom 18. Juni 1935. England und die geheime deutsche Aufrüstung 1933–1935', Phil. Diss. (Bonn, 1972).

N. Wiggershaus, 'Enttarnung der Luftwaffe und Wiedereinführung der allgemeinen Wehrpflicht in Deutschland', *Information für die Truppe*, H.10 (1976) pp. 69–75, 80–3.

M. Wolffsohn, 'Arbeitsbeschaffung und Rüstung im national-sozialistischen Deutschland 1933', *Militärgeschichtliche Mitteilungen*, 22 (1977) pp. 9–21.

G. Wollstein, *Vom Weimarer Revisionismus zu Hitler. Das Deutsche Reich und die Großmächte in der Anfangsphase der nationalsozialistischen Herrschaft in Deutschland* (Bonn, Bad Godesberg, 1973).

H.-G. Zmarzlik, 'Der Sozialdarwinismus in Deutschland als geschichtliches Problem', *Vierteljahrshefte für Zeitgeschichte*, 11 (1963) pp 246–73.

J. Zorach, 'Czechoslovakia's fortifications. Their development and role in the 1938 Munich crisis', *Militärgeschichtliche Mitteilungen*, 20 (1976) pp. 81–94.

Index